# JAVA SWING PROGRAMMING

## GUI TUTORIAL FROM BEGINNER TO EXPERT

## 4 BOOKS IN 1

***BOOK 1***
*JAVA SWING ESSENTIALS: A BEGINNER'S GUIDE TO GUI PROGRAMMING*

***BOOK 2***
*MASTERING JAVA SWING: INTERMEDIATE TECHNIQUES FOR ELEGANT INTERFACES*

***BOOK 3***
*ADVANCED JAVA SWING DEVELOPMENT: BUILDING DYNAMIC AND RESPONSIVE GUIS*

***BOOK 4***
*EXPERT-LEVEL JAVA SWING MASTERY: HARNESSING THE FULL POWER OF GUI PROGRAMMING*

**ROB BOTWRIGHT**

*Published by Rob Botwright*
*Library of Congress Cataloging-in-Publication Data*
*ISBN 978-1-83938-734-0*
*Cover design by Rizzo*

## *Disclaimer*

*The contents of this book are based on extensive research and the best available historical sources. However, the author and publisher make no claims, promises, or guarantees about the accuracy, completeness, or adequacy of the information contained herein. The information in this book is provided on an "as is" basis, and the author and publisher disclaim any and all liability for any errors, omissions, or inaccuracies in the information or for any actions taken in reliance on such information. The opinions and views expressed in this book are those of the author and do not necessarily reflect the official policy or position of any organization or individual mentioned in this book. Any reference to specific people, places, or events is intended only to provide historical context and is not intended to defame or malign any group, individual, or entity. The information in this book is intended for educational and entertainment purposes only. It is not intended to be a substitute for professional advice or judgment. Readers are encouraged to conduct their own research and to seek professional advice where appropriate. Every effort has been made to obtain necessary permissions and acknowledgments for all images and other copyrighted material used in this book. Any errors or omissions in this regard are unintentional, and the author and publisher will correct them in future editions.*

## BOOK 1 - JAVA SWING ESSENTIALS: A BEGINNER'S GUIDE TO GUI PROGRAMMING



## BOOK 2 - MASTERING JAVA SWING: INTERMEDIATE TECHNIQUES FOR ELEGANT INTERFACES



## BOOK 3 - ADVANCED JAVA SWING DEVELOPMENT: BUILDING DYNAMIC AND RESPONSIVE GUIS



## BOOK 4 - EXPERT-LEVEL JAVA SWING MASTERY: HARNESSING THE FULL POWER OF GUI PROGRAMMING

## Introduction

Welcome to the Java Swing Programming bundle, a comprehensive guide that takes you on a journey from beginner to expert in graphical user interface (GUI) programming using Java Swing. Whether you are just starting your journey in GUI development or looking to master advanced techniques, this bundle has something for everyone.

Book 1 - "Java Swing Essentials: A Beginner's Guide to GUI Programming" lays the groundwork for your understanding of Swing. It introduces you to the fundamental concepts, components, and principles of GUI programming in Java, providing you with a solid foundation to build upon.

Book 2 - "Mastering Java Swing: Intermediate Techniques for Elegant Interfaces" takes you to the next level by exploring intermediate techniques and strategies for creating elegant and intuitive interfaces. You will learn advanced layout management, custom component design, and sophisticated event handling to enhance the usability and aesthetics of your applications.

Book 3 - "Advanced Java Swing Development: Building Dynamic and Responsive GUIs" dives deeper into the realm of Swing development, focusing on building dynamic and responsive GUIs. From data visualization to asynchronous processing and advanced event handling, this book equips you with the skills to create highly interactive and engaging user interfaces.

Book 4 - "Expert-level Java Swing Mastery: Harnessing the Full Power of GUI Programming" is your guide to becoming a Swing expert. This book explores advanced topics such as custom painting, animation, and performance optimization, empowering you to leverage the full potential of Swing and build professional-grade applications with confidence.

Whether you are a novice looking to learn the basics or an experienced developer seeking to master advanced techniques, the Java Swing Programming bundle has everything you need to excel in GUI development. Join us on this journey and unlock the power of Java Swing to create stunning and functional graphical interfaces.

***BOOK 1***

***JAVA SWING ESSENTIALS***

***A BEGINNER'S GUIDE TO GUI PROGRAMMING***

***ROB BOTWRIGHT***

## Chapter 1: Introduction to Java Swing

Swing, a powerful GUI toolkit for Java developers, provides a comprehensive framework for building rich and interactive graphical user interfaces (GUIs) in Java applications. With its extensive library of components and robust architecture, Swing offers developers a wide range of tools and functionalities to create visually appealing and user-friendly applications. At its core, Swing is built upon the Java Foundation Classes (JFC) library, which extends the Abstract Window Toolkit (AWT) and provides a platform-independent API for creating GUI components. This allows developers to write code once and deploy it across multiple platforms, making Swing a versatile choice for developing cross-platform applications.

One of the key advantages of Swing is its extensive collection of GUI components, ranging from basic elements like buttons, labels, and text fields to more complex components such as tables, trees, and scroll panes. These components can be easily customized and configured to meet the specific requirements of an application, enabling developers to create highly tailored and visually appealing user interfaces. Moreover, Swing provides support for advanced features such as drag-and-drop functionality, tool tips, and keyboard navigation, allowing developers to enhance the user experience and improve usability.

To get started with Swing development, developers typically begin by setting up their development environment, which involves installing the Java Development Kit (JDK) and configuring an Integrated Development Environment (IDE) such as Eclipse or IntelliJ IDEA. Once the development environment is set up, developers can create a new Swing project and start designing their GUI using the various components provided by Swing. This often involves laying out the components on a JFrame or JPanel using layout managers such as BorderLayout, GridLayout, or GridBagLayout, which help ensure that the GUI looks consistent and is properly aligned across different screen sizes and resolutions.

In addition to its rich set of components, Swing also provides comprehensive support for event handling, allowing developers to respond to user interactions such as button clicks, mouse movements, and keyboard inputs. This is typically done by registering event listeners on the relevant components and implementing callback methods to handle the events. For example, to handle a button click event, developers can add an ActionListener to the button component and implement the actionPerformed method to define the actions to be performed when the button is clicked.

Swing also offers support for internationalization and accessibility, making it easy to develop applications that can be localized into different languages and are accessible to users with disabilities. Developers can use resource bundles to externalize strings and other resources, allowing for easy translation into different languages without modifying the application code. Additionally, Swing provides support for screen readers and other assistive technologies, ensuring that applications are accessible to users with visual impairments or other disabilities.

Furthermore, Swing applications can be deployed using various techniques, depending on the requirements of the project. For standalone desktop applications, developers can package their Swing application into a Java Archive (JAR) file and distribute it to users, who can then run the application on their local machine by executing the JAR file using the java command. Alternatively, Swing applications can be deployed as Java Web Start applications, allowing users to launch the application directly from a web browser without the need for manual installation or updates.

In summary, Swing offers developers a powerful and versatile framework for building GUI applications in Java. With its extensive collection of components, support for advanced features, and cross-platform compatibility, Swing enables developers to create sophisticated and user-friendly applications that can run seamlessly across different operating systems and devices. Whether you're building a simple desktop application or a complex enterprise solution, Swing provides the tools and capabilities you need to bring your ideas to life in the world of Java GUI development.

Java Swing, as a GUI toolkit, offers numerous advantages for developers seeking to build robust and dynamic graphical user interfaces (GUIs) for their Java applications. One of the foremost advantages of using

Java Swing is its platform independence, which allows developers to write code once and deploy it across various operating systems without any modifications. This is made possible by Swing's reliance on the Java Virtual Machine (JVM), which ensures that Swing applications can run on any platform that supports Java, whether it be Windows, macOS, Linux, or others. This platform independence eliminates the need for developers to write separate codebases for different operating systems, streamlining the development process and reducing maintenance overhead.

Additionally, Java Swing offers a rich set of GUI components that enable developers to create highly interactive and visually appealing user interfaces. These components range from basic elements such as buttons, labels, and text fields to more complex components like tables, trees, and tabbed panes, providing developers with the flexibility to design GUIs that meet the specific requirements of their applications. Moreover, Swing components are highly customizable, allowing developers to adjust their appearance, behavior, and functionality to match the desired look and feel of the application. This level of customization enables developers to create unique and branded user interfaces that enhance the overall user experience.

Another key advantage of Java Swing is its comprehensive event handling mechanism, which enables developers to respond to user interactions such as button clicks, mouse movements, and keyboard inputs. This is achieved through the use of event listeners and callback methods, which allow developers to define custom actions to be executed when specific events occur. For example, developers can attach an ActionListener to a button component to handle button click events, or a MouseListener to a component to respond to mouse events such as clicks, drags, and hovers. This event-driven architecture makes it easy to create responsive and interactive GUIs that engage users and provide a seamless user experience.

Furthermore, Java Swing provides robust support for layout management, which simplifies the process of arranging GUI components within a container and ensures that the interface looks consistent across different screen sizes and resolutions. Swing offers a variety of layout managers, including BorderLayout, GridLayout, and GridBagLayout, each with its own strengths and capabilities. These layout managers enable developers to create complex and dynamic layouts that adapt to changes in the application's content and window size, making it easier to design GUIs that are both aesthetically pleasing and functional.

In addition to its rich set of features and functionalities, Java Swing benefits from a large and active community of developers and contributors who provide support, resources, and libraries to help developers build and maintain Swing applications. This vibrant community fosters collaboration and innovation, with developers sharing tips, tutorials, and code snippets to help each other overcome challenges and improve their skills. Additionally, there are numerous third-party libraries and frameworks available for Swing development, offering additional tools and utilities to extend the capabilities of Swing and streamline the development process.

Deploying Java Swing applications is relatively straightforward, thanks to the platform independence of Java. Once the application is developed, it can be packaged into a Java Archive (JAR) file using the jar command-line tool, which bundles the compiled classes, resources, and dependencies into a single executable file. The JAR file can then be distributed to users, who can run the application on their local machine by executing the java command with the path to the JAR file as an argument. Alternatively, Swing applications can be deployed as Java Web Start applications, allowing users to launch the application directly from a web browser without the need for manual installation or updates.

In summary, Java Swing offers developers a powerful and versatile toolkit for building GUI applications in Java. With its platform independence, rich set of components, comprehensive event handling, and robust layout management, Swing enables developers to create sophisticated and user-friendly applications that can run seamlessly across different operating systems and devices. Whether you're building a simple desktop application or a complex enterprise solution, Swing provides the tools and capabilities you need to create compelling and engaging user interfaces that delight users and drive business success.

## Chapter 2: Setting Up Your Development Environment

Installing the Java Development Kit (JDK) is a crucial step for developers looking to build and run Java applications on their local machines. The JDK, provided by Oracle Corporation, includes the Java Runtime Environment (JRE), which is necessary for executing Java applications, as well as additional tools and utilities for compiling, debugging, and profiling Java code. To install the JDK, developers can follow a few simple steps depending on their operating system, starting with downloading the appropriate JDK package from the official Oracle website. For Windows users, the JDK installation process typically involves running the downloaded executable file and following the on-screen instructions provided by the installer. Once the installation is complete, developers can verify the installation by opening a command prompt and executing the java command with the -version option, which displays the installed version of the JDK.

On Linux systems, installing the JDK can be done using package managers such as apt-get on Debian-based distributions or yum on Red Hat-based distributions. For example, on Ubuntu, developers can install the default JDK package by running the following command in the terminal:

arduinoCopy code

```
sudo apt-get install default-jdk
```

This command downloads and installs the default JDK package from the official Ubuntu repositories, which includes the OpenJDK implementation of the Java platform. Once the installation is complete, developers can verify the installation by running the java -version command in the terminal, which should display the installed version of the JDK.

For macOS users, installing the JDK is typically done using the macOS installer package provided by Oracle. After downloading the JDK installer package from the Oracle website, developers can run the installer and follow the on-screen instructions to complete the installation process. Once installed, developers can verify the installation by opening a terminal window and running the java -version command, which should display the installed version of the JDK.

In addition to the JDK itself, developers may also need to set up the Java Development Kit (JDK) is a crucial step for developers looking to build and run Java applications on their local machines. The JDK, provided by Oracle Corporation, includes the Java Runtime Environment (JRE), which is necessary for executing Java applications, as well as additional tools and utilities for compiling, debugging, and profiling Java code. To install the JDK, developers can follow a few simple steps depending on their operating system, starting with downloading the appropriate JDK package from the official Oracle website. For Windows users, the JDK installation process typically involves running the downloaded executable file and following the on-screen instructions provided by the installer. Once the installation is complete, developers can verify the installation by opening a command prompt and executing the java command with the -version option, which displays the installed version of the JDK.

On Linux systems, installing the JDK can be done using package managers such as apt-get on Debian-based distributions or yum on Red Hat-based distributions. For example, on Ubuntu, developers can install the default JDK package by running the following command in the terminal:

arduinoCopy code

```
sudo apt-get install default-jdk
```

This command downloads and installs the default JDK package from the official Ubuntu repositories, which includes the OpenJDK implementation of the Java platform. Once the installation is complete, developers can verify the installation by running the java -version command in the terminal, which should display the installed version of the JDK.

For macOS users, installing the JDK is typically done using the macOS installer package provided by Oracle. After downloading the JDK installer package from the Oracle website, developers can run the installer and follow the on-screen instructions to complete the installation process. Once installed, developers can verify the installation by opening a terminal window and running the java -version command, which should display the installed version of the JDK.

In addition to the JDK itself, developers may also need to set up the JAVA_HOME environment variable, which points to the installation directory of the JDK, and add the JDK's bin directory to the system PATH, which allows the command-line tools provided by the JDK to be executed from any directory. On Windows systems, this can be done by opening the Control Panel, navigating to System and Security > System > Advanced system settings, clicking on the Environment Variables button, and adding a new system variable named JAVA_HOME with the path to the

JDK installation directory. Similarly, on Linux and macOS systems, developers can add the JAVA_HOME environment variable to their shell configuration file (e.g., ~/.bashrc or ~/.bash_profile) and append the JDK's bin directory to the system PATH by modifying the PATH environment variable.

Overall, installing the Java Development Kit (JDK) is an essential prerequisite for Java development, providing developers with the tools and utilities they need to compile, run, and debug Java applications on their local machines. By following the appropriate installation instructions for their operating system and configuring the necessary environment variables, developers can quickly set up their development environment and start writing Java code with ease. Configuring an Integrated Development Environment (IDE) is a crucial step for developers embarking on software development journeys, offering a comprehensive and user-friendly environment for writing, debugging, and deploying code. An IDE serves as a centralized platform where developers can manage their projects, edit source code, and collaborate with team members, streamlining the development process and enhancing productivity. Popular IDEs such as Eclipse, IntelliJ IDEA, and Visual Studio Code provide a wide range of features and tools designed to cater to the needs of developers working in various programming languages and frameworks. To configure an IDE, developers typically start by downloading and installing the IDE software from the official website or package manager of their operating system. For example, to install IntelliJ IDEA on a Windows machine, developers can download the installer executable file from the JetBrains website and run it, following the on-screen instructions provided by the installer. Once installed, developers can launch the IDE and begin the configuration process by setting up their preferences, themes, and key bindings to customize the IDE to their liking. This often involves configuring the appearance and behavior of the IDE's user interface, such as the color scheme, font size, and layout of panels and toolbars. Additionally, developers can install and configure plugins and extensions to extend the functionality of the IDE and integrate it with other tools and services. For instance, developers working with Java can install plugins for Maven, Gradle, and Spring Framework to streamline build and dependency management tasks directly within the IDE. Furthermore, IDEs offer built-in support for version control systems such as Git, enabling developers to commit, push, and pull code changes seamlessly from within the IDE's interface. By configuring the appropriate version control settings and credentials, developers can collaborate with team members and track changes to their codebase efficiently. Another essential aspect of configuring an IDE is setting up project-specific settings and dependencies, such as SDKs, libraries, and build configurations. For example, in IntelliJ IDEA, developers can create a new project and specify the JDK version, language level, and project type (e.g., Java, Kotlin, or Scala) during the project creation wizard. They can then configure additional project settings, such as compiler options, code style preferences, and external dependencies, to ensure consistency and compatibility across the project. Additionally, IDEs offer powerful debugging tools and features to help developers diagnose and fix issues in their code effectively. By configuring breakpoints, watchpoints, and exception handling settings, developers can debug their applications step-by-step, inspecting variables, and evaluating expressions in real-time. Moreover, IDEs provide integration with application servers and deployment platforms, allowing developers to deploy their applications directly from the IDE with minimal effort. For instance, developers working on web applications can configure deployment configurations in IntelliJ IDEA to deploy their applications to Apache Tomcat, JBoss, or other supported servers with just a few clicks. In summary, configuring an Integrated Development Environment (IDE) is an essential task for developers looking to streamline their software development workflow and maximize productivity. By customizing the IDE's settings, preferences, and plugins to suit their needs, developers can create a personalized and efficient development environment tailored to their unique requirements. With its comprehensive features and tools, an IDE serves as a powerful platform for writing, debugging, and deploying code, empowering developers to build high-quality software with confidence and ease.

## Chapter 3: Understanding Swing Components

Exploring Basic Swing Components in Java provides developers with a foundational understanding of the fundamental building blocks for creating graphical user interfaces (GUIs) in Java applications. Swing, a part of the Java Foundation Classes (JFC), offers a wide range of GUI components that developers can leverage to design intuitive and interactive user interfaces for their applications. These components include buttons, labels, text fields, check boxes, radio buttons, and more, each serving a specific purpose and functionality in the GUI.
To get started with exploring basic Swing components, developers typically begin by setting up their development environment, which involves installing the Java Development Kit (JDK) and configuring an Integrated Development Environment (IDE) such as Eclipse, IntelliJ IDEA, or NetBeans. Once the development environment is set up, developers can create a new Java project and import the necessary Swing libraries to their project's classpath, allowing them to access and use the Swing components in their code.

One of the most common Swing components is the JButton, which represents a standard push button that users can click to perform an action. To create a JButton in Java, developers can instantiate a new instance of the JButton class and specify the text label for the button.

For example, the following Java code creates a simple JButton with the text label "Click Me":

javaCopy code

```
import javax.swing.*; public class Main { public static void main(String[] args) { JFrame frame = new JFrame("Basic Swing Components"); JButton button = new JButton("Click Me"); frame.getContentPane().add(button); frame.setDefaultCloseOperation(JFrame.EXIT_ON_CLOSE); frame.pack(); frame.setVisible(true); } }
```

This code creates a new JFrame window with the title "Basic Swing Components" and adds a JButton with the text label "Click Me" to the frame's content pane. The frame's default close operation is set to EXIT_ON_CLOSE, which exits the application when the user closes the window. Finally, the pack() and setVisible(true) methods are called to resize the frame to fit its components and make the frame visible on the screen, respectively.

In addition to buttons, Swing provides JLabels for displaying text or images on the GUI. JLabels are often used to provide descriptive labels or instructions to users in the interface. To create a JLabel in Java, developers can instantiate a new instance of the JLabel class and specify the text or icon to be displayed. For example, the following code creates a JLabel with the text "Hello, World!" and adds it to the frame's content pane:

javaCopy code

JLabel label = new JLabel("Hello, World!"); frame.getContentPane().add(label);

Similarly, developers can use JTextFields to allow users to input text into the GUI. JTextFields are commonly used for collecting user input, such as entering a username or password. To create a JTextField in Java, developers can instantiate a new instance of the JTextField class and optionally specify the initial text and column width. For example, the following code creates a JTextField with an initial text "Enter your name" and a column width of 20:

javaCopy code

JTextField textField = new JTextField("Enter your name", 20); frame.getContentPane().add(textField);

Furthermore, Swing provides JCheckBoxes and JRadioButtons for allowing users to make selections from a list of options. JCheckBoxes represent checkboxes that users can toggle on or off, while JRadioButtons represent radio buttons that allow users to select one option from a group of mutually exclusive options. To create JCheckBoxes and JRadioButtons in Java, developers can instantiate new instances of the JCheckBox and JRadioButton classes and specify the text label for each option. For example, the following code creates a group of JRadioButtons representing different colors:

javaCopy code

JRadioButton redButton = new JRadioButton("Red"); JRadioButton greenButton = new JRadioButton("Green"); JRadioButton blueButton =

```
new JRadioButton("Blue"); ButtonGroup colorGroup
= new ButtonGroup(); colorGroup.add(redButton);
colorGroup.add(greenButton);
colorGroup.add(blueButton);
frame.getContentPane().add(redButton);
frame.getContentPane().add(greenButton);
frame.getContentPane().add(blueButton);
```

In summary, exploring basic Swing components in Java provides developers with a solid foundation for building GUIs for their applications. By understanding how to create and use components such as buttons, labels, text fields, checkboxes, and radio buttons, developers can design intuitive and interactive user interfaces that enhance the overall user experience. With its rich library of GUI components and comprehensive documentation, Swing remains a popular choice for Java developers seeking to create cross-platform desktop applications with ease.

Understanding container components in Java Swing is essential for developers aiming to create complex and well-structured graphical user interfaces (GUIs) for their applications. Container components play a pivotal role in organizing and managing the layout of other GUI components, such as buttons, labels, and text fields, within a GUI window. In Swing, a container is a component that can hold and manage other components, known as child components or subcomponents, allowing developers to arrange and position them in a hierarchical structure. By understanding the various types of container components and their respective layout managers, developers can create flexible and responsive GUI layouts that adapt to different screen sizes and resolutions. To get started with understanding container components in Swing, developers typically begin by exploring the different types of container classes provided by the Swing library, such as JFrame, JPanel, and JDialog. These classes serve as the building blocks for creating GUI windows and dialog boxes in Swing applications, each offering unique features and functionalities for organizing and displaying GUI components. For example, JFrame is a top-level container that represents the main window of a Swing application, while JPanel is a lightweight container that can be nested within other containers to create more complex layouts. To create a JFrame window in Java Swing, developers can instantiate a new instance of the JFrame class and add GUI components to its content pane. For example, the following code creates a simple JFrame window with a JButton and a JLabel:

javaCopy code

```
import javax.swing.*; public class Main { public static void main(String[] args) { JFrame frame = new JFrame("Understanding Container Components"); JButton button = new JButton("Click Me"); JLabel label = new JLabel("Hello, World!");
frame.getContentPane().add(button);
frame.getContentPane().add(label);
```

```
frame.setDefaultCloseOperation(JFrame.EXIT_ON_CLO
SE); frame.pack(); frame.setVisible( true ); } }
```

In this code, a new JFrame window with the title "Understanding Container Components" is created, and a JButton with the text "Click Me" and a JLabel with the text "Hello, World!" are added to the frame's content pane. The frame's default close operation is set to EXIT_ON_CLOSE, which exits the application when the user closes the window. Finally, the pack() and setVisible(true) methods are called to resize the frame to fit its components and make the frame visible on the screen, respectively.

Apart from JFrame, JPanel is another commonly used container component in Swing, providing developers with a lightweight and versatile container for organizing GUI components. Unlike JFrame, which represents a standalone window, JPanel can be used to group related components together and manage their layout independently. Developers can add JPanel instances to JFrame windows or nest them within other JPanel instances to create more complex GUI layouts. To create a JPanel in Java Swing, developers can instantiate a new instance of the JPanel class and add GUI components to it. For example, the following code creates a JPanel with a JTextField and a JButton nested within it:

javaCopy code

```
JPanel panel = new JPanel(); JTextField textField =
new JTextField( 20 ); JButton button = new
```

```
JButton("Submit");        panel.add(textField);
panel.add(button);
```

In this code, a new JPanel instance is created, and a JTextField and a JButton are added to the panel using the add() method. The JTextField is configured with a column width of 20, specifying the number of characters visible in the text field at a time. By adding components to JPanel instances and arranging them using layout managers, developers can create complex and dynamic GUI layouts that adapt to changes in the application's content and window size.

Furthermore, Swing provides several layout manager classes that developers can use to control the arrangement and positioning of GUI components within container components. Layout managers are responsible for determining the size and location of child components within a container, ensuring that they are displayed correctly on the screen. Some of the commonly used layout managers in Swing include BorderLayout, FlowLayout, GridLayout, and GridBagLayout, each offering different capabilities and constraints for arranging components. For example, BorderLayout arranges components in five regions: North, South, East, West, and Center, while FlowLayout arranges components in a single row or column, wrapping them to the next row or column as needed. By choosing the appropriate layout manager for their GUI layout, developers can achieve the desired look and feel for their applications and ensure that components are displayed consistently across different screen sizes and resolutions.

In summary, understanding container components in Java Swing is essential for developers seeking to create flexible and responsive GUI layouts for their applications. By leveraging container classes such as JFrame and JPanel and using layout managers to arrange GUI components, developers can create intuitive and visually appealing user interfaces that enhance the overall user experience. With its rich library of container components and layout managers, Swing remains a popular choice for Java developers looking to build cross-platform desktop applications with ease.

## Chapter 4: Basic GUI Design Principles

Understanding the principles of user interface design is essential for creating effective and user-friendly graphical user interfaces (GUIs) that meet the needs and expectations of users. These principles, often referred to as heuristics, guidelines, or best practices, serve as a framework for designing interfaces that are intuitive, efficient, and satisfying to use. By following these principles, developers can create interfaces that facilitate user interaction, minimize cognitive load, and promote user engagement. One of the fundamental principles of user interface design is the principle of consistency, which states that interfaces should be consistent in their layout, terminology, and behavior across different parts of the application. Consistency helps users develop mental models of how the interface works, making it easier for them to navigate and use the application. To achieve consistency in interface design, developers should use standard conventions and patterns, such as placing navigation menus at the top of the screen and using familiar icons for common actions. Additionally, developers should use consistent terminology and labels to describe interface elements and actions, avoiding jargon or ambiguous language that may confuse users. Another important principle of user interface design is the principle of feedback, which states that interfaces should provide feedback to users to confirm their actions and inform them of the system's state. Feedback can take various forms, such as visual cues, audio signals, or text messages, depending on the context of the interaction. For example, when users click a button or submit a form, the interface should provide visual feedback, such as changing the appearance of the button or displaying a progress indicator, to indicate that the action has been recognized and is being processed. Similarly, when users encounter errors or issues, the interface should provide clear and informative error messages to help them understand the problem and how to resolve it. Moreover, the principle of affordance is crucial in user interface design, referring to the perceptual cues that suggest how users can interact with interface elements. Affordances help users understand the functionality and purpose of interface elements at a glance, reducing the need for explicit instructions or explanations. For example, buttons with a raised appearance suggest that they can be clicked, while text fields with a cursor indicate that they can be edited. By designing interface elements with clear affordances, developers can make the interface more intuitive and user-friendly, enabling users to interact with confidence and efficiency. Additionally, the principle of simplicity emphasizes the importance of keeping interfaces simple and streamlined, avoiding unnecessary complexity or clutter that may overwhelm or confuse users. Simple interfaces are easier to understand and navigate, reducing the cognitive load on users and increasing their satisfaction and enjoyment. To achieve simplicity in interface design, developers should prioritize essential features and content, removing any unnecessary elements or distractions that do not contribute to the user's goals. This may involve decluttering the interface, using white space to create visual breathing room, and organizing content in a logical and hierarchical manner. Furthermore, the principle of user control highlights the importance of giving users control over their interactions with the interface, allowing them to navigate, explore, and customize the interface according to their preferences and needs. User control can be achieved through various means, such as providing clear navigation options, offering customization settings, and supporting undo and redo actions. By empowering users with control over their interactions, developers can create interfaces that adapt to individual preferences and workflows, enhancing user satisfaction and engagement. Moreover, the principle of accessibility underscores the importance of designing interfaces that are accessible to users with disabilities or impairments, ensuring that all users can access and use the interface effectively. Accessibility features include providing alternative text for images, supporting keyboard navigation, and offering adjustable font sizes and color schemes. By designing interfaces with accessibility in mind, developers can create inclusive and equitable experiences for all users, regardless of their abilities or limitations. In summary, understanding the principles of user interface design is essential for creating interfaces that are intuitive, efficient, and satisfying to use. By following principles such as consistency, feedback, affordance, simplicity, user control, and accessibility, developers can design interfaces that facilitate user interaction, minimize cognitive load, and promote user engagement. By prioritizing user needs and preferences in the design process, developers can create interfaces that deliver exceptional user experiences and drive the success of their applications.

Applying consistency and feedback in GUI design is fundamental to creating interfaces that are intuitive, user-friendly, and effective in facilitating user interaction. Consistency in GUI design refers to the uniformity of elements, layout, and behavior throughout the interface, ensuring that users can easily understand and navigate the application. One way to apply consistency in GUI design is by maintaining a consistent visual style, including color schemes, typography, and iconography, across all screens and components of the interface. This helps users develop mental models of how the interface works and reduces cognitive load by eliminating the need to learn new design patterns or conventions for different parts of the application. Additionally, consistency in terminology and labeling is crucial for ensuring that users can understand and interpret interface elements consistently across different contexts. For example, using the same terminology and labels for similar actions or features helps users recognize and predict the behavior of interface elements, making the interface more predictable and easier to use.

Furthermore, feedback in GUI design plays a vital role in providing users with confirmation of their actions and informing them of the system's response to their input.

Feedback can take various forms, including visual, auditory, or tactile cues, depending on the nature of the interaction and the context of the application. One common form of feedback in GUI design is visual feedback, which involves changing the appearance or state of interface elements in response to user actions. For example, when users hover over a clickable element such as a button or link, the element may change color or display a tooltip to indicate that it is interactive. Similarly, when users click a button or submit a form, the interface should provide immediate visual feedback, such as a loading spinner or progress bar, to indicate that the action has been recognized and is being processed. This helps users feel in control of their interactions with the interface and reduces uncertainty or anxiety about whether their actions have been successfully executed.

Moreover, auditory feedback can be used to complement visual feedback in GUI design, providing additional cues to users about the status or outcome of their actions. For example, when users perform an action that requires confirmation, such as deleting a file or submitting a form, the interface may play a sound effect to indicate success or failure. Similarly, when users encounter errors or issues, the interface may play an error sound or beep to alert them to the problem and prompt them to take corrective action. Auditory feedback can be particularly useful in situations where visual feedback may be overlooked or inaccessible, such as for users with visual impairments or in environments with high levels of ambient noise.

Additionally, tactile feedback can be employed in GUI design to provide users with physical sensations or vibrations in response to their actions. Tactile feedback is commonly used in touch-based interfaces, such as smartphones and tablets, where users can feel a vibration or haptic feedback when tapping on virtual buttons or interacting with touch-sensitive controls. This tactile feedback helps users confirm their actions and provides a more engaging and immersive user experience.

To apply consistency and feedback in GUI design effectively, developers should consider the principles of usability and user-centered design, focusing on the needs, expectations, and preferences of the target audience. This may involve conducting user research, such as usability testing and user interviews, to understand how users interact with the interface and identify areas for improvement. Additionally, developers should iterate on the design based on feedback from users and stakeholders, refining the interface to address usability issues and enhance the overall user experience. By applying consistency and feedback in GUI design, developers can create interfaces that are intuitive, efficient, and satisfying to use, ultimately driving user engagement and success for the application.

## Chapter 5: Event Handling in Swing

Event-driven programming in Swing is a fundamental concept that underpins the development of graphical user interfaces (GUIs) in Java applications, allowing developers to create dynamic and interactive interfaces that respond to user input and system events. In event-driven programming, the flow of the program is driven by events, which are generated by user actions, such as clicking a button or typing text, or by system events, such as window resizing or data loading. These events trigger event handlers, which are methods or functions that are executed in response to specific events, allowing developers to define custom behavior for different scenarios. In Swing, event-driven programming is facilitated by the Java Event-Dispatching Thread (EDT), which is responsible for processing and dispatching events to the appropriate event handlers. The EDT ensures that GUI components are updated and manipulated in a thread-safe manner, preventing concurrency issues and ensuring a responsive user interface.

To implement event-driven programming in Swing, developers typically start by creating GUI components, such as buttons, text fields, and labels, and adding event listeners to these components to handle user interactions. Event listeners are interfaces or classes that define callback methods for handling specific types of events, such as ActionListener for handling button clicks or ItemListener for handling checkbox selections. For example, to handle button clicks in Swing, developers can add an ActionListener to a JButton component and implement the actionPerformed() method to define the behavior to be executed when the button is clicked. The following code demonstrates how to create a JButton with an ActionListener in Swing:

javaCopy code

```
import javax.swing.*; import java.awt.event.*; public class Main { public static void main(String[] args) { JFrame frame = new JFrame("Event-Driven Programming in Swing"); JButton button = new JButton("Click Me"); button.addActionListener(new ActionListener() { public void actionPerformed(ActionEvent e) { JOptionPane.showMessageDialog(frame, "Button clicked!"); } }); frame.getContentPane().add(button); frame.setDefaultCloseOperation(JFrame.EXIT_ON_CLO
SE); frame.pack(); frame.setVisible(true); } }
```

In this example, an ActionListener is added to the JButton component using the addActionListener() method, which takes an ActionListener object as an argument. Inside the actionPerformed() method of the ActionListener, a JOptionPane dialog is displayed to show a message when the button is clicked.

Moreover, Swing provides a variety of event listener interfaces and adapter classes that developers can use to handle different types of events, such as MouseEvent for mouse events, KeyEvent for keyboard events, and

WindowEvent for window events. For example, to handle mouse clicks on a component in Swing, developers can add a MouseListener to the component and implement the mouseClicked() method to define the behavior to be executed when the mouse is clicked. Similarly, to handle keyboard input in Swing, developers can add a KeyListener to a component and implement the keyPressed() method to handle key presses.

In addition to handling user interactions, event-driven programming in Swing also allows developers to respond to system events, such as window resizing, window closing, or data loading. Swing provides event listener interfaces and adapter classes for these types of events, such as ComponentListener for component events and WindowListener for window events. For example, to handle window closing events in Swing, developers can add a WindowListener to a JFrame component and implement the windowClosing() method to define the behavior to be executed when the window is closed. The following code demonstrates how to add a WindowListener to a JFrame component in Swing:

javaCopy code

```
frame.addWindowListener(new WindowAdapter() { public void windowClosing(WindowEvent e) { // Perform cleanup or save operations before closing the window System.exit(0); } });
```

In this example, a WindowAdapter is added to the JFrame component using the addWindowListener() method, and the windowClosing() method is overridden to define the behavior to be executed when the window is closed.

Furthermore, event-driven programming in Swing allows developers to implement custom event types and event listeners to handle application-specific events. This can be useful for implementing communication between different components of the application or for implementing custom user interactions. To define custom event types in Swing, developers can create subclasses of the java.util.EventObject class and define additional fields and methods to represent the event data. They can then create custom event listener interfaces or classes that extend the java.util.EventListener interface and define methods for handling the custom events.

Overall, event-driven programming in Swing is a powerful paradigm for creating dynamic and interactive GUIs in Java applications. By leveraging event listeners and event handling mechanisms provided by Swing, developers can create interfaces that respond to user input and system events in real-time, providing a rich and engaging user experience. Event-driven programming enables developers to decouple the logic for handling events from the code for creating and updating GUI components, making it easier to maintain and extend the application's functionality. By mastering event-driven programming in Swing, developers can create GUIs that are both functional and intuitive, meeting the needs and expectations of users.

Registering and handling events is a fundamental aspect

of software development, particularly in event-driven programming paradigms like Java Swing, where user interaction plays a crucial role in application behavior. In Java Swing, events are actions or occurrences that happen during the execution of a program, such as clicking a button, typing text, or resizing a window. Handling events involves defining code that responds to these events, enabling developers to create dynamic and interactive user interfaces. To effectively handle events in Java Swing, developers need to understand how to register event listeners, define event handling methods, and implement event-driven logic. One common approach to registering event listeners in Java Swing is by using the addActionListener() method, which allows developers to attach an ActionListener to a component, such as a JButton, JTextField, or JMenuItem, to listen for specific events, such as button clicks or menu selections. For example, to register an ActionListener for a JButton in Java Swing, developers can use the following code snippet:

javaCopy code

```java
button.addActionListener(new ActionListener() { public void actionPerformed(ActionEvent e) { // Event handling logic goes here } });
```

In this code snippet, an anonymous inner class implementing the ActionListener interface is passed as an argument to the addActionListener() method of the JButton component. Inside the actionPerformed() method of the ActionListener interface, developers can define the code that should be executed when the button is clicked. This allows developers to encapsulate event handling logic within the ActionListener implementation, keeping the code organized and modular.

Moreover, event listeners in Java Swing can also be registered using lambda expressions, which provide a more concise and readable syntax for defining event handling logic. For example, the previous code snippet can be rewritten using lambda expressions as follows:

javaCopy code

```
button.addActionListener(e -> { // Event handling logic goes here });
```

In this version, the ActionListener interface is implemented using a lambda expression, which simplifies the syntax and reduces boilerplate code. Lambda expressions are particularly useful for handling simple events or actions where only a few lines of code are needed.

Additionally, Java Swing provides a wide range of predefined listener interfaces for handling different types of events, such as ActionListeners for handling button clicks, KeyListeners for handling keyboard input, MouseListeners for handling mouse events, and ItemListeners for handling item selections in checkboxes and radio buttons. By implementing these listener interfaces and overriding their corresponding event handling methods, developers can define custom event handling logic for specific events.

For example, to handle button clicks in Java Swing using a KeyListener, developers can implement the keyPressed() method of the KeyListener interface to respond to key presses, as shown in the following code snippet:

javaCopy code

```
button.addKeyListener(new KeyListener() { public void keyPressed(KeyEvent e) { // Check if the Enter key was pressed if (e.getKeyCode() == KeyEvent.VK_ENTER) { // Event handling logic goes here } } public void keyReleased(KeyEvent e) { // Unused method } public void keyTyped(KeyEvent e) { // Unused method } });
```

In this example, the keyPressed() method of the KeyListener interface checks if the Enter key was pressed (identified by the KeyEvent.VK_ENTER constant) and executes the event handling logic accordingly.

Furthermore, event handling in Java Swing often involves updating the state or appearance of GUI components in response to user actions or system events. For example, when a button is clicked, developers may want to update a JLabel to display a message, change the color of a JPanel, or enable/disable other components in the interface. To achieve this, developers can use methods provided by Swing components to modify their properties dynamically. For example, to change the text of a JLabel in response to a button click, developers can use the setText() method of the JLabel component, as shown in the following code snippet:

javaCopy code

```
button.addActionListener(e -> { label.setText("Button clicked!"); });
```

In this code snippet, the setText() method of the JLabel component is called inside the ActionListener to change the text displayed by the label when the button is clicked.

Moreover, event handling in Java Swing often involves coordinating interactions between multiple components and managing the flow of the application based on user input. For example, developers may need to validate user input, update the state of the interface dynamically, or trigger other actions or events in response to specific user interactions. To achieve this, developers can use control structures such as if statements, switch statements, loops, and conditional expressions to implement complex event-driven logic. By combining event listeners, GUI components, and control structures effectively, developers can create dynamic and responsive user interfaces that meet the requirements and expectations of users.

Additionally, Java Swing provides support for event propagation and event delegation, allowing events to be propagated from child components to parent components and vice versa. This enables developers to define event handlers at different levels of the component hierarchy, providing flexibility and modularity in event-driven programming. For example, events generated by child components, such as buttons or text fields, can be handled by their parent container or by higher-level components in the hierarchy, allowing developers to encapsulate event handling logic at different levels of abstraction.

In summary, registering and handling events in Java Swing is a fundamental aspect of GUI programming, enabling developers to create dynamic and interactive user interfaces that respond to user input and system events. By understanding how to register event listeners, define event handling methods, and implement event-driven logic effectively, developers can create robust and responsive applications that provide a rich and engaging user experience. By leveraging the event-driven programming model provided by Java Swing, developers can build GUI applications that are intuitive, efficient, and satisfying to use, ultimately enhancing user satisfaction and driving the success of their projects.

## Chapter 6: Layout Management in Java Swing

Layout managers are an essential aspect of graphical user interface (GUI) development, dictating how components are arranged and sized within a container. In Java Swing, layout managers play a crucial role in designing flexible and responsive user interfaces that adapt to different screen sizes and resolutions. When creating GUIs in Swing, developers have the option to use various layout managers to organize and position components, each offering different strategies for managing component layout and alignment. One of the most commonly used layout managers in Swing is the BorderLayout manager, which divides the container into five regions: north, south, east, west, and center. To use BorderLayout in Swing, developers can simply add components to the container and specify the desired region using the add() method. For example, the following code demonstrates how to create a JFrame with BorderLayout in Swing:

javaCopy code

import javax.swing.*; public class Main { public static void main(String[] args) { JFrame frame = new JFrame("Introduction to Layout Managers"); JButton button1 = new JButton("North"); JButton button2 = new JButton("South"); JButton button3 = new JButton("East"); JButton button4 = new JButton("West"); JButton button5 = new

```
JButton ( "Center" );
frame.getContentPane().add(button1,
BorderLayout.NORTH);
frame.getContentPane().add(button2,
BorderLayout.SOUTH);
frame.getContentPane().add(button3,
BorderLayout.EAST);
frame.getContentPane().add(button4,
BorderLayout.WEST);
frame.getContentPane().add(button5,
BorderLayout.CENTER);
frame.setDefaultCloseOperation(JFrame.EXIT_ON_CLO
SE); frame.pack(); frame.setVisible( true ); } }
```

In this example, buttons are added to the JFrame using the add() method, with each button specified to be positioned in a different region of the BorderLayout. The frame is then set to exit on close, packed to fit its components, and made visible. Another commonly used layout manager in Swing is the FlowLayout manager, which arranges components in a left-to-right, top-to-bottom flow. To use FlowLayout in Swing, developers can simply add components to the container, and they will be automatically arranged according to the flow direction. For example, the following code demonstrates how to create a JFrame with FlowLayout in Swing:

javaCopy code

```
import javax.swing.*; public class Main { public static void main(String[] args) { JFrame frame = new
```

```
JFrame("Introduction to Layout Managers"); JButton
button1 = new JButton("Button 1"); JButton button2
= new JButton("Button 2"); JButton button3 = new
JButton("Button 3"); JButton button4 = new
JButton("Button 4"); JButton button5 = new
JButton("Button 5");
frame.getContentPane().setLayout(new FlowLayout());
frame.getContentPane().add(button1);
frame.getContentPane().add(button2);
frame.getContentPane().add(button3);
frame.getContentPane().add(button4);
frame.getContentPane().add(button5);
frame.setDefaultCloseOperation(JFrame.EXIT_ON_CLO
SE); frame.pack(); frame.setVisible(true); } }
```

In this example, buttons are added to the JFrame using the add() method without specifying any layout constraints, allowing them to be arranged automatically by the FlowLayout manager. The frame is then set to exit on close, packed to fit its components, and made visible. Additionally, Swing provides other layout managers, such as GridLayout, BoxLayout, and GridBagLayout, each offering different capabilities and flexibility for organizing components. For example, GridLayout arranges components in a grid of rows and columns, with each component occupying a single cell, while BoxLayout arranges components in a single row or column, allowing for more flexible alignment and spacing. GridBagLayout is the most flexible and powerful layout manager in Swing, allowing developers to specify constraints for each component to control its position, size, and alignment within the container. To use GridBagLayout in Swing, developers can create a GridBagConstraints object to define the layout constraints for each component and add the component to the container using the add() method with the GridBagConstraints object as an argument. Overall, understanding layout managers is essential for creating well-designed and responsive GUIs in Swing, enabling developers to create interfaces that adapt to different screen sizes and resolutions and provide a consistent and intuitive user experience. By choosing the appropriate layout manager for their application and understanding how to use it effectively, developers can create GUIs that meet the needs and expectations of users and enhance the overall usability and accessibility of their applications.

Choosing the right layout manager for your application is a critical decision in the development process, as it directly impacts the organization and presentation of graphical user interface (GUI) components. In Java Swing, the choice of layout manager determines how components are arranged within containers, affecting the overall look and feel of the application and influencing its usability and user experience. With a variety of layout managers available in Swing, each offering different capabilities and flexibility, selecting the most suitable layout manager requires careful consideration of factors such as the application's design requirements, the type and complexity of the user interface, and the target platform and device. One commonly used layout manager in Swing is the BorderLayout manager, which divides the container into five regions: north, south, east, west, and center. This layout manager is well-suited for applications with a simple and straightforward layout, where components are organized into distinct regions of the window, such as toolbars, menus, and content areas. To use BorderLayout in Swing, developers can simply add components to the container and specify the desired region using the add() method. For example, the following code demonstrates how to create a JFrame with BorderLayout in Swing:

javaCopy code

```
import javax.swing.*; public class Main { public static void main(String[] args) { JFrame frame = new JFrame("Choosing the Right Layout Manager"); JButton button1 = new JButton("North"); JButton button2 = new JButton("South"); JButton button3 = new JButton("East"); JButton button4 = new JButton("West"); JButton button5 = new JButton("Center");
frame.getContentPane().add(button1,
BorderLayout.NORTH);
frame.getContentPane().add(button2,
BorderLayout.SOUTH);
frame.getContentPane().add(button3,
BorderLayout.EAST);
frame.getContentPane().add(button4,
```

```
BorderLayout.WEST);
frame.getContentPane().add(button5,
BorderLayout.CENTER);
frame.setDefaultCloseOperation(JFrame.EXIT_ON_CLO
SE); frame.pack(); frame.setVisible( true ); } }
```

In this example, buttons are added to the JFrame using the add() method, with each button specified to be positioned in a different region of the BorderLayout. The frame is then set to exit on close, packed to fit its components, and made visible. Another commonly used layout manager in Swing is the GridLayout manager, which arranges components in a grid of rows and columns, with each component occupying a single cell. GridLayout is suitable for applications that require a uniform grid layout, such as forms, tables, and grids, where components are aligned in rows and columns. To use GridLayout in Swing, developers can specify the number of rows and columns in the grid and add components to the container using the add() method. For example, the following code demonstrates how to create a JFrame with GridLayout in Swing:

javaCopy code

```
import javax.swing.*; public class Main { public static
void main(String[] args) { JFrame frame = new
JFrame( "Choosing the Right Layout Manager" ); JPanel
panel = new JPanel( new GridLayout( 2, 2)); JButton
button1 = new JButton( "Button 1" ); JButton button2
= new JButton( "Button 2" ); JButton button3 = new
JButton( "Button 3" ); JButton button4 = new
```

```
JButton("Button 4"); panel.add(button1);
panel.add(button2); panel.add(button3);
panel.add(button4);
frame.getContentPane().add(panel);
frame.setDefaultCloseOperation(JFrame.EXIT_ON_CLO
SE); frame.pack(); frame.setVisible(true); } }
```

In this example, a JPanel is created with a GridLayout of 2 rows and 2 columns, and buttons are added to the panel using the add() method. The panel is then added to the JFrame's content pane, and the frame is set to exit on close, packed to fit its components, and made visible. Additionally, Swing provides other layout managers, such as FlowLayout, BoxLayout, and GridBagLayout, each offering different capabilities and flexibility for organizing components. FlowLayout arranges components in a left-to-right, top-to-bottom flow, making it suitable for applications with a flexible and dynamic layout. BoxLayout arranges components in a single row or column, allowing for more flexible alignment and spacing. GridBagLayout is the most flexible and powerful layout manager in Swing, allowing developers to specify constraints for each component to control its position, size, and alignment within the container. To choose the right layout manager for your application, consider factors such as the complexity and structure of the user interface, the requirements for flexibility and responsiveness, and the compatibility with the target platform and device. Experiment with different layout managers to find the one that best meets your application's design requirements and provides the desired user experience. By choosing the right layout manager for your application, you can create GUIs that are well-organized, visually appealing, and easy to use, enhancing the overall usability and user satisfaction of your application.

## Chapter 7: Working with Text and Labels

Displaying text with JLabel is a fundamental aspect of graphical user interface (GUI) development in Java Swing, providing a simple and versatile way to present static text to users within a GUI component. JLabel is a Swing component that allows developers to display text, images, or both, providing various formatting options and customization capabilities to meet the design requirements of the application. To display text with JLabel in Swing, developers can create an instance of the JLabel class, set the desired text using the setText() method, and add the JLabel to a container such as a JFrame or JPanel. For example, the following code demonstrates how to create a JFrame with a JLabel displaying static text in Swing:

javaCopy code

```
import javax.swing.*; public class Main { public static void main(String[] args) { JFrame frame = new JFrame("Displaying Text with JLabel"); JLabel label = new JLabel("Hello, World!"); frame.getContentPane().add(label); frame.setDefaultCloseOperation(JFrame.EXIT_ON_CLOSE); frame.pack(); frame.setVisible(true); } }
```

In this example, a JLabel with the text "Hello, World!" is created and added to the JFrame's content pane using the add() method. The frame is then set to exit on close, packed to fit its components, and made visible. JLabel also supports HTML formatting, allowing developers to display text with custom styles, fonts, colors, and alignments. To use HTML formatting with JLabel, developers can set the text using HTML tags and specify the desired formatting within the tags. For example, the following code demonstrates how to create a JLabel with HTML-formatted text in Swing:

javaCopy code

```
import javax.swing.*; public class Main { public static
void main(String[] args) { JFrame frame = new
JFrame("Displaying Text with JLabel"); JLabel label =
new JLabel("<html><h1 style='color: blue;'>Welcome to
Swing</h1><p>This is a JLabel with HTML-formatted
text.</p></html>"); frame.getContentPane().add(label);
frame.setDefaultCloseOperation(JFrame.EXIT_ON_CLOSE)
; frame.pack(); frame.setVisible(true); } }
```

In this example, a JLabel with HTML-formatted text is created and added to the JFrame's content pane. The text includes an HTML <h1> heading with blue color and a <p> paragraph tag. The frame is then set to exit on close, packed to fit its components, and made visible. Additionally, JLabel supports displaying images alongside text, allowing developers to create more visually rich and dynamic interfaces. To display an image with JLabel in Swing, developers can create an ImageIcon object with the desired image file and set it as the icon for the JLabel using the setIcon() method. For example, the following code demonstrates how to create a JLabel with an image in Swing:

javaCopy code

```
import javax.swing.*; public class Main { public static
void main(String[] args) { JFrame frame = new
```

```
JFrame("Displaying Text with JLabel"); ImageIcon icon = new ImageIcon("image.png"); JLabel label = new JLabel("Hello, World!", icon, JLabel.CENTER); frame.getContentPane().add(label); frame.setDefaultCloseOperation(JFrame.EXIT_ON_CLOSE); frame.pack(); frame.setVisible(true); } }
```

In this example, an ImageIcon object with the image file "image.png" is created, and a JLabel with the text "Hello, World!" and the image icon is created. The JLabel is aligned to the center using the JLabel.CENTER alignment constant. The frame is then set to exit on close, packed to fit its components, and made visible. JLabel provides various methods and properties for customizing the appearance and behavior of the text, such as setting the font, color, alignment, and border. Developers can use these methods to create visually appealing and informative labels that enhance the usability and aesthetics of their applications. By mastering the techniques for displaying text with JLabel in Swing, developers can create GUIs that effectively communicate information to users and provide a seamless and intuitive user experience.

Editing text with JTextComponent is a fundamental aspect of developing text-based applications in Java Swing, providing developers with powerful tools for creating and manipulating text within graphical user interfaces (GUIs). JTextComponent is an abstract class in Swing that serves as the base class for various text components, such as JTextArea, JTextField, and JTextPane, each offering different features and capabilities for editing and displaying text. JTextComponent provides a rich set of methods and properties for working with text, allowing developers to perform operations such as inserting, deleting, selecting, and formatting text, as well as handling user input and managing text attributes. To use JTextComponent in Swing, developers can create an instance of a concrete subclass, configure its properties as needed, and add it to a container such as a JFrame or JPanel. For example, the following code demonstrates how to create a JFrame with a JTextArea for editing text in Swing:

javaCopy code

```
import javax.swing.*; public class Main { public static void main(String[] args) { JFrame frame = new JFrame("Editing Text with JTextComponent"); JTextArea textArea = new JTextArea(); JScrollPane scrollPane = new JScrollPane(textArea); frame.getContentPane().add(scrollPane); frame.setDefaultCloseOperation(JFrame.EXIT_ON_CLOSE); frame.pack(); frame.setVisible(true); } }
```

In this example, a JTextArea is created and wrapped in a JScrollPane to provide scrolling functionality for large amounts of text. The JTextArea is then added to the JFrame's content pane using the add() method. The frame is set to exit on close, packed to fit its components, and made visible. JTextComponent provides various methods for manipulating text, such as setText() to set the text content, getText() to retrieve the text content, and append() to add text to the end of the document. For example, the following code demonstrates how to set and retrieve text content from a JTextArea in Swing:

javaCopy code

```
import javax.swing.*; public class Main { public static void main(String[] args) { JFrame frame = new JFrame("Editing Text with JTextComponent"); JTextArea textArea = new JTextArea(); textArea.setText("Hello, World!"); String text = textArea.getText(); System.out.println("Text content: " + text); frame.getContentPane().add(textArea); frame.setDefaultCloseOperation(JFrame.EXIT_ON_CLOSE); frame.pack(); frame.setVisible(true); } }
```

In this example, the setText() method is used to set the text content of the JTextArea to "Hello, World!". The getText() method is then called to retrieve the text content from the JTextArea, which is printed to the console. JTextComponent also provides methods for selecting text, such as setSelectionStart() and setSelectionEnd() to set the selection range, and getSelectedText() to retrieve the selected text. For example, the following code demonstrates how to select and retrieve text from a JTextArea in Swing:

javaCopy code

```
import javax.swing.*; public class Main { public static void main(String[] args) { JFrame frame = new JFrame("Editing Text with JTextComponent"); JTextArea textArea = new JTextArea(); textArea.setText("Hello, World!"); textArea.setSelectionStart(0); textArea.setSelectionEnd(5); String selectedText = textArea.getSelectedText(); System.out.println("Selected text: " + selectedText);
```

```
frame.getContentPane().add(textArea);
frame.setDefaultCloseOperation(JFrame.EXIT_ON_CLOSE)
; frame.pack(); frame.setVisible(true); } }
```

In this example, the setText() method is used to set the text content of the JTextArea to "Hello, World!". The setSelectionStart() and setSelectionEnd() methods are then called to select the text range from index 0 to index 5. The getSelectedText() method is used to retrieve the selected text, which is printed to the console. JTextComponent also supports various keyboard and mouse events for handling user input, such as key presses, mouse clicks, and text selection. Developers can register event listeners and implement event handler methods to respond to these events and perform custom actions, such as validating input, formatting text, or updating the user interface. Overall, JTextComponent is a versatile and powerful class in Swing for editing and displaying text within GUIs, offering a wide range of features and capabilities for creating text-based applications. By mastering the techniques for working with JTextComponent, developers can create rich and interactive user interfaces that effectively communicate information and provide a seamless and intuitive user experience.

## Chapter 8: Buttons and ActionListeners

Creating buttons with JButton is a fundamental aspect of graphical user interface (GUI) development in Java Swing, providing developers with a simple yet powerful tool for adding interactive elements to their applications. JButton is a Swing component that represents a clickable button, allowing users to trigger actions or events by clicking on the button. In Swing, JButton provides various features and customization options for creating buttons with different styles, sizes, and functionalities to meet the design requirements of the application. To create buttons with JButton in Swing, developers can create an instance of the JButton class, set the desired text or icon using the setText() or setIcon() methods, and add event listeners to handle button clicks. For example, the following code demonstrates how to create a JFrame with a JButton in Swing:

javaCopy code

```
import javax.swing.*; public class Main { public static void main(String[] args) { JFrame frame = new JFrame("Creating Buttons with JButton"); JButton button = new JButton("Click Me"); frame.getContentPane().add(button); frame.setDefaultCloseOperation(JFrame.EXIT_ON_CLOSE); frame.pack(); frame.setVisible( true ); } }
```

In this example, a JButton with the text "Click Me" is created and added to the JFrame's content pane using the add() method. The frame is then set to exit on close, packed to fit its components, and made visible. JButton supports various properties and methods for customizing the appearance and behavior of buttons, such as setEnabled() to enable or disable the button, setToolTipText() to set a tooltip for the button, and setPreferredSize() to set the preferred size of the button. For example, the following code demonstrates how to create a disabled button with a tooltip in Swing:

javaCopy code

```
import javax.swing.*; public class Main { public static void main(String[] args) { JFrame frame = new JFrame("Creating Buttons with JButton"); JButton button = new JButton("Click Me"); button.setEnabled(false); button.setToolTipText("This button is disabled"); frame.getContentPane().add(button); frame.setDefaultCloseOperation(JFrame.EXIT_ON_CLOSE); frame.pack(); frame.setVisible(true); } }
```

In this example, a JButton with the text "Click Me" is created and configured to be disabled using the setEnabled() method. A tooltip is also set for the button using the setToolTipText() method. The frame is then set to exit on close, packed to fit its components, and made visible. JButton also supports displaying icons alongside text on buttons, allowing developers to create more visually appealing and informative buttons. To display an icon with text on a JButton in Swing, developers can create an instance of the ImageIcon class with the desired image file and set it as the icon for the button using the setIcon() method. For example, the following code demonstrates how to create a JButton with an icon in Swing:

javaCopy code

```
import javax.swing.*; public class Main { public static void main(String[] args) { JFrame frame = new JFrame("Creating Buttons with JButton"); ImageIcon icon = new ImageIcon("icon.png"); JButton button = new JButton("Click Me", icon); frame.getContentPane().add(button); frame.setDefaultCloseOperation(JFrame.EXIT_ON_CLOSE); frame.pack(); frame.setVisible(true); } }
```

In this example, an ImageIcon object with the image file "icon.png" is created, and a JButton with the text "Click Me" and the icon is created. The button is then added to the JFrame's content pane, and the frame is set to exit on close, packed to fit its components, and made visible. Additionally, JButton supports registering event listeners to handle button clicks and perform custom actions in response to user interactions. Developers can add ActionListener objects to buttons using the addActionListener() method and implement the actionPerformed() method to define the behavior to be executed when the button is clicked. For example, the following code demonstrates how to create a JButton with an ActionListener in Swing:

javaCopy code

```
import javax.swing.*; import java.awt.event.*; public class Main { public static void main(String[] args) { JFrame frame = new JFrame("Creating Buttons with JButton"); JButton button = new JButton("Click Me"); button.addActionListener(new ActionListener() { public void actionPerformed(ActionEvent e) { JOptionPane.showMessageDialog(frame, "Button clicked!"); } }); frame.getContentPane().add(button); frame.setDefaultCloseOperation(JFrame.EXIT_ON_CLOSE); frame.pack(); frame.setVisible(true); } }
```

In this example, an ActionListener is added to the JButton using the addActionListener() method, and the actionPerformed() method is implemented to show a message dialog when the button is clicked. The frame is then set to exit on close, packed to fit its components, and made visible. Overall, JButton is a versatile and powerful component in Swing for creating interactive buttons in GUI applications, offering a wide range of features and customization options for building intuitive and engaging user interfaces. By mastering the techniques for working with JButton, developers can create buttons that effectively communicate actions to users and provide a seamless and intuitive user experience.

Handling button clicks with ActionListener is a fundamental aspect of developing interactive graphical user interfaces (GUIs) in Java Swing, enabling developers to respond to user actions and trigger specific behaviors or events when buttons are clicked.

In Swing, ActionListener is an interface that defines a single method, actionPerformed(), which is invoked when an action event occurs, such as clicking on a button. By implementing the ActionListener interface and registering action listeners to buttons, developers can define custom actions or event handlers to be executed when buttons are clicked, allowing for dynamic and responsive user interactions in GUI applications. To handle button clicks with ActionListener in Swing, developers can create a class that implements the ActionListener interface and implements the actionPerformed() method to define the desired behavior. For example, the following code demonstrates how to create a JFrame with a JButton and handle button clicks with ActionListener in Swing:

javaCopy code

```
import javax.swing.*; import java.awt.event.*; public class Main { public static void main(String[] args) { JFrame frame = new JFrame("Handling Button Clicks with ActionListener"); JButton button = new JButton("Click Me"); button.addActionListener(new ActionListener() { public void actionPerformed(ActionEvent e) { JOptionPane.showMessageDialog(frame, "Button clicked!"); } }); frame.getContentPane().add(button); frame.setDefaultCloseOperation(JFrame.EXIT_ON_CLOSE); frame.pack(); frame.setVisible(true); } }
```

In this example, an ActionListener is added to the JButton using the addActionListener() method, and the actionPerformed() method is implemented to show a message dialog when the button is clicked. The frame is then set to exit on close, packed to fit its components, and made visible. ActionListener allows developers to define custom actions or event handlers for buttons, enabling a wide range of possibilities for responding to user interactions in GUI applications. For example, developers can use ActionListener to perform data validation, trigger calculations or computations, update the user interface, navigate to different screens or views, or invoke external services or APIs. By encapsulating the desired behavior within the actionPerformed() method, developers can create modular and maintainable code that is easy to understand and extend. Additionally, ActionListener provides flexibility and reusability, allowing the same action listener implementation to be reused across multiple buttons or components within the same application or across different applications. For example, developers can create a single ActionListener implementation for handling common actions such as saving data, deleting records, or submitting forms, and register this action listener to multiple buttons or components as needed. This promotes code consistency and reduces duplication, leading to cleaner and more efficient codebases. Furthermore, ActionListener supports event-driven programming, which is a key paradigm in GUI development where actions or events triggered by user interactions drive the flow and behavior of the application. By registering action listeners to buttons and other interactive components, developers can create applications that respond dynamically to user input, providing a more engaging and intuitive user experience. However, it's essential to consider best practices when handling button clicks with ActionListener to ensure the reliability, efficiency, and usability of the application. For example, developers should strive to keep actionPerformed() method implementations concise and focused on a single responsibility to maintain readability and ease of maintenance. Additionally, developers should handle exceptions gracefully within the actionPerformed() method to prevent crashes or unexpected behavior and provide informative error messages or feedback to users when necessary. Furthermore, developers should consider accessibility requirements when designing GUIs and ensure that button click actions are accessible to users with disabilities, such as providing keyboard shortcuts or alternative input methods for triggering actions. By following best practices and guidelines for handling button clicks with ActionListener, developers can create robust, user-friendly GUI applications that meet the needs and expectations of users. In summary, ActionListener is a powerful and versatile interface in Java Swing for handling button clicks and responding to user actions in GUI applications. By leveraging ActionListener, developers can create interactive and responsive user interfaces that enhance the overall usability and user experience of their applications.

## Chapter 9: Handling User Input with Text Fields and Text Areas

Accepting single-line input with JTextField is a fundamental aspect of developing user input functionality in Java Swing, offering developers a straightforward way to capture textual input from users within graphical user interfaces (GUIs). JTextField is a Swing component that provides a text editing field, allowing users to enter and edit single-line text input. This component is widely used in various GUI applications, such as forms, search bars, login screens, and more, enabling users to input textual data easily and efficiently. To accept single-line input with JTextField in Swing, developers can create an instance of the JTextField class, configure its properties as needed, and add it to a container such as a JFrame or JPanel. For example, the following code demonstrates how to create a JFrame with a JTextField for accepting single-line input in Swing:

javaCopy code

```
import javax.swing.*; public class Main { public static void main(String[] args) { JFrame frame = new JFrame("Accepting Single Line Input with JTextField"); JTextField textField = new JTextField(20); frame.getContentPane().add(textField); frame.setDefaultCloseOperation(JFrame.EXIT_ON_CLOSE); frame.pack(); frame.setVisible(true); } }
```

In this example, a JTextField with a width of 20 columns is created and added to the JFrame's content pane using the add() method. The frame is then set to exit on close, packed to fit its components, and made visible. JTextField provides various properties and methods for customizing the appearance and behavior of the text field, such as setText() to set the initial text content, getText() to retrieve the text content, and setEditable() to enable or disable text editing. For example, the following code demonstrates how to create a JTextField with an initial text value and disable text editing in Swing:

javaCopy code

```
import javax.swing.*; public class Main { public static void main(String[] args) { JFrame frame = new JFrame("Accepting Single Line Input with JTextField"); JTextField textField = new JTextField(20); textField.setText("Initial Value"); textField.setEditable(false); frame.getContentPane().add(textField); frame.setDefaultCloseOperation(JFrame.EXIT_ON_CLOSE); frame.pack(); frame.setVisible(true); } }
```

In this example, a JTextField with a width of 20 columns is created and configured with an initial text value of "Initial Value" using the setText() method. The setEditable() method is then called to disable text editing for the text field. The frame is set to exit on close, packed to fit its components, and made visible. Additionally, JTextField supports event listeners for capturing user input and responding to text changes in real-time. Developers can register DocumentListener objects to text fields using the getDocument().addDocumentListener() method and implement the methods defined in the DocumentListener interface to handle text insertions, removals, and updates. For example, the following code demonstrates how to create a JTextField with a DocumentListener for capturing text changes in Swing:

javaCopy code

```
import javax.swing.*; import javax.swing.event.*; public class Main { public static void main(String[] args) { JFrame frame = new JFrame("Accepting Single Line Input with JTextField"); JTextField textField = new JTextField(20); textField.getDocument().addDocumentListener(new DocumentListener() { public void insertUpdate(DocumentEvent e) { System.out.println("Text inserted: " + textField.getText()); } public void removeUpdate(DocumentEvent e) { System.out.println("Text removed: " + textField.getText()); } public void changedUpdate(DocumentEvent e) { // Not used for plain text components } }); frame.getContentPane().add(textField); frame.setDefaultCloseOperation(JFrame.EXIT_ON_CLOSE); frame.pack(); frame.setVisible(true); } }
```

In this example, a JTextField with a width of 20 columns is created, and a DocumentListener is added to the text field using the getDocument().addDocumentListener() method. The insertUpdate() and removeUpdate() methods defined in the DocumentListener interface are implemented to handle text insertions and removals, respectively. When text is inserted or removed in the text field, the corresponding methods are invoked, printing the updated text content to the console. The frame is set to exit on close, packed to fit its components, and made visible. JTextField is a versatile component in Swing for accepting single-line input from users in GUI applications. By leveraging its properties, methods, and event listeners, developers can create intuitive and interactive user interfaces that facilitate data entry and user interaction. Whether used for simple data entry fields or more complex input forms, JTextField provides a flexible and efficient solution for capturing textual input in Java Swing applications.

Accepting multiline input with JTextArea is essential for developing Java Swing applications that require users to input and edit text spanning multiple lines, offering developers a versatile and powerful component for capturing longer-form textual content within graphical user interfaces (GUIs). JTextArea is a Swing component that provides a multi-line text editing area, enabling users to enter and manipulate text across multiple lines, making it suitable for various use cases such as text editors, chat applications, note-taking apps, and more. To accept multiline input with JTextArea in Swing, developers can create an instance of the JTextArea class, configure its properties as needed, and add it to a container such as a JFrame or JScrollPane for scrolling functionality. For example, the following code demonstrates how to create a JFrame with a JTextArea for accepting multiline input in Swing:

javaCopy code

```
import javax.swing.*; public class Main { public static void main(String[] args) { JFrame frame = new JFrame("Accepting Multiline Input with JTextArea"); JTextArea textArea = new JTextArea(10, 30); JScrollPane scrollPane = new JScrollPane(textArea); frame.getContentPane().add(scrollPane); frame.setDefaultCloseOperation(JFrame.EXIT_ON_CLOSE); frame.pack(); frame.setVisible(true); } }
```

In this example, a JTextArea with 10 rows and 30 columns is created, and it is wrapped in a JScrollPane to provide scrolling functionality for large amounts of text. The JTextArea is then added to the JFrame's content pane using the add() method. The frame is set to exit on close, packed to fit its components, and made visible. JTextArea provides various properties and methods for customizing the appearance and behavior of the text area, such as setText() to set the initial text content, getText() to retrieve the text content, and setLineWrap() to enable or disable automatic line wrapping. For example, the following code demonstrates how to create a JTextArea with an initial text value and enable automatic line wrapping in Swing:

javaCopy code

```
import javax.swing.*; public class Main { public static void main(String[] args) { JFrame frame = new JFrame("Accepting Multiline Input with JTextArea"); JTextArea textArea = new JTextArea(10, 30); textArea.setText("Initial text value"); textArea.setLineWrap(true); JScrollPane scrollPane = new JScrollPane(textArea); frame.getContentPane().add(scrollPane); frame.setDefaultCloseOperation(JFrame.EXIT_ON_CLOSE); frame.pack(); frame.setVisible(true); } }
```

In this example, a JTextArea with 10 rows and 30 columns is created, and it is configured with an initial text value of "Initial text value" using the setText() method. The setLineWrap() method is then called to enable automatic line wrapping for the text area. The JTextArea is wrapped in a JScrollPane to provide scrolling functionality, and the scroll pane is added to the JFrame's content pane. The frame is set to exit on close, packed to fit its components, and made visible. JTextArea also supports event listeners for capturing user input and responding to text changes in real-time. Developers can register DocumentListener objects to text areas using the getDocument().addDocumentListener() method and implement the methods defined in the DocumentListener interface to handle text insertions, removals, and updates. For example, the following code demonstrates how to create a JTextArea with a DocumentListener for capturing text changes in Swing:

javaCopy code

```
import javax.swing.*; import javax.swing.event.*; public class Main { public static void main(String[] args) { JFrame frame = new JFrame("Accepting Multiline Input with JTextArea"); JTextArea textArea = new JTextArea(10, 30); textArea.getDocument().addDocumentListener(new DocumentListener() { public void insertUpdate(DocumentEvent e) { System.out.println("Text inserted: " + textArea.getText()); } public void removeUpdate(DocumentEvent e) { System.out.println("Text removed: " + textArea.getText()); } public void changedUpdate(DocumentEvent e) { // Not used for plain text components } }); JScrollPane scrollPane = new JScrollPane(textArea); frame.getContentPane().add(scrollPane); frame.setDefaultCloseOperation(JFrame.EXIT_ON_CLOSE); frame.pack(); frame.setVisible(true); } }
```

In this example, a JTextArea with 10 rows and 30 columns is created, and a DocumentListener is added to the text area using the getDocument().addDocumentListener() method. The insertUpdate() and removeUpdate() methods defined in the DocumentListener interface are implemented to handle text insertions and removals, respectively. When text is inserted or removed in the text area, the corresponding methods are invoked, printing the updated text content to the console. The JTextArea is wrapped in a JScrollPane to provide scrolling functionality, and the scroll pane is added to the JFrame's content pane. The frame is set to exit on close, packed to fit its components, and made visible. JTextArea is a versatile component in Swing for accepting multiline input from users in GUI applications. By leveraging its properties, methods, and event listeners, developers can create intuitive and interactive user interfaces that facilitate data entry and user interaction across multiple lines of text. Whether used for simple text entry fields or more complex text editing and manipulation tasks, JTextArea provides a flexible and efficient solution for capturing longer-form textual input in Java Swing applications.

## Chapter 10: Introduction to Swing Menus and Toolbars

Creating menus with JMenuBar is an essential aspect of developing graphical user interfaces (GUIs) in Java Swing, offering developers a versatile and intuitive way to organize and present application functionality in a hierarchical menu structure. JMenuBar is a Swing component that serves as a container for menu bars in Swing applications, providing a platform-independent and customizable solution for incorporating menus into GUIs. By leveraging JMenuBar, developers can create menu bars with menus, submenus, and menu items, allowing users to access various commands, options, and features of the application with ease. To create menus with JMenuBar in Swing, developers can create an instance of the JMenuBar class, add JMenu objects representing individual menus, and add JMenuItem objects representing menu items to the menus as needed. For example, the following code demonstrates how to create a JFrame with a JMenuBar containing menus and menu items in Swing:

javaCopy code

```
import javax.swing.*; public class Main { public static void main(String[] args) { JFrame frame = new JFrame("Creating Menus with JMenuBar"); JMenuBar menuBar = new JMenuBar(); JMenu fileMenu = new JMenu("File"); JMenuItem newMenuItem = new JMenuItem("New"); JMenuItem openMenuItem =
```

```
new JMenuItem("Open"); JMenuItem saveMenuItem
= new JMenuItem("Save"); JMenuItem exitMenuItem
= new JMenuItem("Exit");
fileMenu.add(newMenuItem);
fileMenu.add(openMenuItem);
fileMenu.add(saveMenuItem);
fileMenu.addSeparator(); fileMenu.add(exitMenuItem);
menuBar.add(fileMenu);
frame.setJMenuBar(menuBar); frame.setSize(400,
300);
frame.setDefaultCloseOperation(JFrame.EXIT_ON_CLO
SE); frame.setVisible(true); } }
```

In this example, a JFrame with a title "Creating Menus with JMenuBar" is created. A JMenuBar object is instantiated, and a JMenu object representing the "File" menu is created. JMenuItem objects representing menu items such as "New," "Open," "Save," and "Exit" are also created and added to the "File" menu. A separator is added between the "Save" and "Exit" menu items using the addSeparator() method. Finally, the "File" menu is added to the JMenuBar, and the JMenuBar is set as the menu bar of the JFrame using the setJMenuBar() method. The JFrame is sized, set to exit on close, and made visible. JMenuBar supports various properties and methods for customizing the appearance and behavior of menu bars, menus, and menu items. For example, developers can use setMnemonic() to assign keyboard mnemonics to menu items, setAccelerator() to assign keyboard shortcuts, and setIcon() to set icons for menu items. Additionally, JMenuBar supports event listeners for handling user interactions with menus and menu items. Developers can register ActionListener objects to menu items using the addActionListener() method and implement the actionPerformed() method to define the actions to be performed when menu items are selected. For example, the following code demonstrates how to create a JMenuItem with an ActionListener in Swing:

javaCopy code

```
import javax.swing.*; import java.awt.event.*; public class Main { public static void main(String[] args) { JFrame frame = new JFrame("Creating Menus with JMenuBar"); JMenuBar menuBar = new JMenuBar(); JMenu fileMenu = new JMenu("File"); JMenuItem exitMenuItem = new JMenuItem("Exit"); exitMenuItem.addActionListener(new ActionListener() { public void actionPerformed(ActionEvent e) { System.exit(0); } }); fileMenu.add(exitMenuItem); menuBar.add(fileMenu);
frame.setJMenuBar(menuBar); frame.setSize(400, 300);
frame.setDefaultCloseOperation(JFrame.EXIT_ON_CLOSE); frame.setVisible(true); } }
```

In this example, an ActionListener is added to the "Exit" menu item using the addActionListener() method. When the "Exit" menu item is selected, the actionPerformed() method is invoked, and the System.exit() method is called with an argument of 0 to terminate the application. The JFrame is sized, set to exit on close, and made visible. Overall, JMenuBar provides a flexible and powerful mechanism for creating menus in Java Swing applications, enabling developers to organize and present application functionality in a user-friendly and intuitive manner. By leveraging JMenuBar, developers can enhance the usability and accessibility of their applications, providing users with easy access to commands, options, and features through hierarchical menu structures. Whether used for simple menus with basic functionality or more complex menus with nested submenus and dynamic menu items, JMenuBar offers a robust and customizable solution for incorporating menus into Swing GUIs.

Adding toolbars to your Swing application is a crucial aspect of enhancing user interaction and providing quick access to frequently used features and commands, offering developers a convenient way to integrate buttons, icons, and other components into the application's graphical user interface (GUI). In Swing, a toolbar is typically positioned at the top or sides of the application window, allowing users to perform common actions with ease without navigating through menus or dialog boxes. To add toolbars to your Swing application, you can use the JToolBar class, which provides a flexible and customizable container for holding various components such as buttons, toggle buttons, text fields, and separators. One way to create a toolbar in Swing is by creating an instance of JToolBar, adding the desired components to it, and then adding the toolbar to the application window's content pane. For example, the following code demonstrates how to create a simple toolbar with buttons in a Swing application:

javaCopy code

```
import javax.swing.*; public class Main { public static void main(String[] args) { JFrame frame = new JFrame("Adding Toolbars to Your Swing Application"); JToolBar toolBar = new JToolBar(); JButton newButton = new JButton("New"); JButton openButton = new JButton("Open"); JButton saveButton = new JButton("Save"); toolBar.add(newButton); toolBar.add(openButton); toolBar.add(saveButton); frame.getContentPane().add(toolBar); frame.setSize(400, 300); frame.setDefaultCloseOperation(JFrame.EXIT_ON_CLOSE); frame.setVisible(true); } }
```

In this example, a JFrame with the title "Adding Toolbars to Your Swing Application" is created. A JToolBar object named toolBar is instantiated, and three JButton objects representing "New," "Open," and "Save" buttons are created and added to the toolbar using the add() method. The toolbar is then added to the content pane of the JFrame, which is sized, set to exit on close, and made visible. JToolBar supports various properties and methods for customizing the appearance and behavior of toolbars. For instance, you can use setFloatable() to specify whether the toolbar can be dragged and floated as a separate window, setRollover() to enable or disable button rollover effects, and setOrientation() to set the orientation of the toolbar (horizontal or vertical). Additionally, JToolBar allows you to add separators between components to visually group related buttons or provide visual breaks between different sections of the toolbar. You can add separators using the addSeparator() method. For example, the following code demonstrates how to add separators to a toolbar in Swing:

javaCopy code

```
import javax.swing.*; public class Main { public static void main(String[] args) { JFrame frame = new JFrame("Adding Toolbars to Your Swing Application"); JToolBar toolBar = new JToolBar(); JButton newButton = new JButton("New"); JButton openButton = new JButton("Open"); JButton saveButton = new JButton("Save"); toolBar.add(newButton); toolBar.addSeparator(); toolBar.add(openButton); toolBar.addSeparator(); toolBar.add(saveButton); frame.getContentPane().add(toolBar); frame.setSize(400, 300); frame.setDefaultCloseOperation(JFrame.EXIT_ON_CLOSE); frame.setVisible(true); } }
```

In this example, separators are added between the "New," "Open," and "Save" buttons using the addSeparator() method. This creates visual gaps between the buttons, making the toolbar more visually appealing and easier to navigate. Toolbars in Swing applications can also include icons alongside text labels to provide visual cues and improve usability. You can use ImageIcon objects to load and display images for toolbar buttons. For example, the following code demonstrates how to add icons to toolbar buttons in Swing:

javaCopy code

```
import javax.swing.*; public class Main { public static void main(String[] args) { JFrame frame = new JFrame("Adding Toolbars to Your Swing Application"); JToolBar toolBar = new JToolBar(); ImageIcon newIcon = new ImageIcon("new.png"); ImageIcon openIcon = new ImageIcon("open.png"); ImageIcon saveIcon = new ImageIcon("save.png"); JButton newButton = new JButton("New", newIcon); JButton openButton = new JButton("Open", openIcon); JButton saveButton = new JButton("Save", saveIcon); toolBar.add(newButton); toolBar.add(openButton); toolBar.add(saveButton); frame.getContentPane().add(toolBar); frame.setSize(400, 300); frame.setDefaultCloseOperation(JFrame.EXIT_ON_CLOSE); frame.setVisible(true); } }
```

In this example, ImageIcon objects are created using image files named "new.png," "open.png," and "save.png" located in the application's directory. These icons are then passed as arguments to the JButton constructors along with the button labels. When the toolbar is displayed, the buttons will have both text labels and icons, providing users with both visual and textual cues for each action. Overall, adding toolbars to your Swing application is a powerful way to enhance user interaction and streamline access to application features and commands. By leveraging the JToolBar class and its associated components, developers can create intuitive and visually appealing toolbars that improve the overall usability and accessibility of their applications. Whether used for simple actions or more complex workflows, toolbars play a crucial role in designing effective and user-friendly Swing interfaces.

***BOOK 2***
***MASTERING JAVA SWING***
***INTERMEDIATE TECHNIQUES FOR ELEGANT INTERFACES***

***ROB BOTWRIGHT***

Advanced JList configuration allows developers to harness the full potential of this Swing component, enabling them to create highly customized and interactive list-based user interfaces in Java applications. JList is a versatile component for displaying lists of items in GUIs, offering various features for data presentation, selection handling, and custom rendering. To achieve advanced configurations with JList, developers can utilize techniques such as custom cell rendering, handling complex data models, implementing drag-and-drop functionality, and customizing selection behavior. One essential aspect of advanced JList configuration is custom cell rendering, which enables developers to customize the appearance of individual list cells based on the data they represent. By implementing custom cell renderers, developers can control how each item in the list is visually presented to the user, allowing for sophisticated and visually appealing displays. To implement custom cell rendering in JList, developers can create a custom subclass of DefaultListCellRenderer or implement the ListCellRenderer interface. This custom renderer can then be set on the JList using the setCellRenderer() method. For example, the following code demonstrates how to create a custom cell renderer to display items with different foreground colors based on their values:
javaCopy code

```
import javax.swing.*; import java.awt.*; import java.util.*; public class CustomCellRenderer extends DefaultListCellRenderer { private static final Map<String, Color> COLORS = new HashMap<>(); static { COLORS.put("Red", Color.RED); COLORS.put("Green", Color.GREEN); COLORS.put("Blue", Color.BLUE); } @Override public Component getListCellRendererComponent(JList<?> list, Object value, int index, boolean isSelected, boolean cellHasFocus) { JLabel label = (JLabel) super.getListCellRendererComponent(list, value, index, isSelected, cellHasFocus); String text = value.toString();
label.setForeground(COLORS.getOrDefault(text,
Color.BLACK)); return label; } }
```

In this example, a custom cell renderer is created by subclassing DefaultListCellRenderer. The getListCellRendererComponent() method is overridden to customize the appearance of list cells based on their values. The text color of each cell is set based on a predefined map of colors. The custom cell renderer can then be set on a JList instance using the setCellRenderer() method to apply the custom rendering to the list. Another aspect of advanced JList configuration is handling complex data models, allowing developers to manage and manipulate the data displayed in the list efficiently. In Swing, the data model for a JList is typically represented by an instance of the ListModel interface, which defines methods for accessing and manipulating the list data. For more complex scenarios, developers can create custom implementations of the ListModel interface to support dynamic data updates, filtering, and sorting. Additionally, developers can leverage the DefaultListModel class, which provides a basic implementation of ListModel backed by a mutable list of objects. This allows for easy manipulation of list data through methods such as addElement(), removeElement(), and removeAllElements(). For example, the following code demonstrates how to create a JList with a custom data model using DefaultListModel:

javaCopy code

```
import javax.swing.*; public class Main { public static void main(String[] args) { JFrame frame = new JFrame("Advanced JList Configuration"); DefaultListModel<String> model = new DefaultListModel<>(); model.addElement("Item 1"); model.addElement("Item 2"); model.addElement("Item 3"); JList<String> list = new JList<>(model); frame.getContentPane().add(new JScrollPane(list)); frame.setSize(400, 300); frame.setDefaultCloseOperation(JFrame.EXIT_ON_CLOSE); frame.setVisible(true); } }
```

In this example, a DefaultListModel<String> is created and populated with three items. The list model is then passed as an argument to the JList constructor, resulting in a JList instance with the specified data model. The list is wrapped in a JScrollPane for scrollable functionality and added to the JFrame's content pane. When working with complex data models, developers may also need to implement custom cell editors and listeners to handle data updates and user interactions appropriately. Additionally, advanced JList configuration may involve implementing drag-and-drop functionality to allow users to reorder items within the list or transfer items between multiple lists. Swing provides built-in support for drag-and-drop operations through the TransferHandler class, which enables developers to define drag-and-drop behavior for JList components. To enable drag-and-drop functionality for a JList, developers can create a custom TransferHandler and set it on the list using the setTransferHandler() method. The TransferHandler can then handle drag-and-drop events and perform operations such as moving or copying list items. For example, the following code demonstrates how to implement drag-and-drop functionality for a JList:

javaCopy code

```
import javax.swing.*; import java.awt.*; import java.awt.datatransfer.*; import java.awt.dnd.*; public class Main { public static void main(String[] args) { JFrame frame = new JFrame("Advanced JList Configuration"); DefaultListModel<String> model = new DefaultListModel<>(); model.addElement("Item 1"); model.addElement("Item 2"); model.addElement("Item 3"); JList<String> list = new JList<>(model); list.setDragEnabled(true);
```

```
list.setDropMode(DropMode.INSERT); TransferHandler handler = new TransferHandler() { @Override public boolean canImport(TransferSupport support) { return support.isDataFlavorSupported(DataFlavor.stringFlavor); } @Override public boolean importData(TransferSupport support) { try { String data = (String) support.getTransferable().getTransferData(DataFlavor.stringFlavor); JList.DropLocation dl = (JList.DropLocation) support.getDropLocation(); int index = dl.getIndex(); model.add(index, data); return true; } catch (UnsupportedFlavorException | IOException e) { e.printStackTrace(); return false; } } };
list.setTransferHandler(handler);
frame.getContentPane().add(new JScrollPane(list));
frame.setSize(400, 300);
frame.setDefaultCloseOperation(JFrame.EXIT_ON_CLOSE); frame.setVisible(true); } }
```

In this example, drag-and-drop functionality is enabled for the JList by setting its dragEnabled property to true. Additionally, the drop mode is set to INSERT to allow items to be dropped between existing items in the list. A custom TransferHandler is created to handle drag-and-drop events. The canImport() method determines whether the data can be imported, and the importData() method performs the actual data import operation. When a drag-and-drop operation occurs, the TransferHandler extracts the transferred data (in this case, a string) and inserts it into the list at the appropriate position. Finally, the TransferHandler is set on the JList using the setTransferHandler() method to enable drag-and-drop functionality. Overall, advanced JList configuration allows developers to create highly customized and interactive list-based user interfaces in Java Swing applications. By leveraging techniques such as custom cell rendering, complex data modeling, drag-and-drop functionality, and more, developers

Creating custom JTable renderers is a fundamental skill for Java Swing developers, allowing them to tailor the visual representation of table cells to suit specific application requirements and enhance the user experience. JTable is a versatile component for displaying tabular data in Swing applications, providing developers with extensive customization options for cell rendering, editing, and formatting. By creating custom cell renderers, developers can control how data is displayed within table cells, including customizing fonts, colors, icons, and other visual elements. To create a custom cell renderer in Swing, developers typically subclass the DefaultTableCellRenderer class or implement the TableCellRenderer interface to define custom rendering logic for table cells. This custom renderer can then be applied to specific columns or cells within the JTable to achieve the desired visual effects. One common use case for custom cell renderers is displaying data in a format that differs from the default string representation. For example, developers may need to display numerical values as currency, percentages, or dates, or they may want to display images or icons within table cells. To achieve this, developers can create custom cell renderers that format the data accordingly and render it with the desired visual appearance. For example, the following code demonstrates how to create a custom cell renderer to display numerical values as currency:

javaCopy code

```
import javax.swing.*; import javax.swing.table.*; import java.awt.*; import java.text.*; public class CurrencyCellRenderer extends DefaultTableCellRenderer { private static final NumberFormat CURRENCY_FORMAT = NumberFormat.getCurrencyInstance(); @Override protected void setValue(Object value) { if (value != null && value instanceof Number) { setText(CURRENCY_FORMAT.format(value)); } else { super.setValue(value); } } }
```

In this example, a custom cell renderer named CurrencyCellRenderer is created by subclassing DefaultTableCellRenderer. The setValue() method is overridden to format numerical values as currency using NumberFormat.getCurrencyInstance(). When the renderer is applied to a JTable column, it will automatically format numerical cell values as currency. Another use case for custom cell renderers is displaying images or icons within table cells to represent data visually. For example, developers may want to display status indicators, icons representing file types, or thumbnail images within a table. To achieve this, developers can create custom cell renderers that render ImageIcon or Image objects within table cells. For example, the following code demonstrates how to create a custom cell renderer to display ImageIcon objects within table cells:

javaCopy code

```
import javax.swing.*; import javax.swing.table.*; import java.awt.*; public class ImageCellRenderer extends DefaultTableCellRenderer { @Override protected void setValue(Object value) { if (value != null && value instanceof ImageIcon) { setIcon((ImageIcon) value); setText(""); } else { super.setValue(value); } } }
```

In this example, a custom cell renderer named ImageCellRenderer is created by subclassing DefaultTableCellRenderer. The setValue() method is overridden to set the icon of the renderer to the specified ImageIcon object. When the renderer is applied to a JTable column containing ImageIcon objects, it will display the icons within the table cells. Additionally, developers can create more complex custom cell renderers to achieve advanced rendering effects, such as rendering cells with custom colors, fonts, borders, or background images. By customizing the rendering behavior of JTable cells, developers can create visually appealing and informative table-based user interfaces that effectively communicate data to users. Furthermore, custom cell renderers can be combined with other JTable features, such as cell editors, row sorters, and table models, to create powerful and interactive data-driven applications. When deploying applications with custom JTable renderers, developers should ensure that the renderers are applied to the appropriate columns or cells within the JTable to achieve the desired visual effects. This can be done by setting the appropriate cell renderer for each column using the TableColumn.setCellRenderer() method or by implementing a custom TableCellRenderer that applies different rendering logic based on the cell's row and column indices. Additionally, developers should consider performance implications when using custom cell renderers, especially for large tables with a large number of rows or columns. Custom renderers that perform complex rendering operations or rely on external resources such as images or icons may impact the responsiveness and efficiency of the application, so it's essential to test the performance of custom renderers in real-world usage scenarios and optimize them as needed. Overall, creating custom JTable renderers is a valuable skill for Java Swing developers, enabling them to create visually appealing and user-friendly table-based interfaces that effectively present and communicate data to users. By leveraging custom renderers, developers can tailor the appearance of table cells to match the specific requirements and design goals of their applications, resulting in a more polished and professional user experience.

## Chapter 2: Customizing Look and Feel

Customizing UI components with UIManager is an essential technique for Java Swing developers, enabling them to modify the look and feel of their applications to match specific design requirements and branding guidelines. UIManager is a powerful tool that provides a centralized mechanism for configuring and customizing the appearance and behavior of Swing components, including buttons, text fields, scroll bars, borders, and more. By adjusting UIManager properties and installing custom look and feel (L&F) themes, developers can achieve a consistent and visually appealing user interface across their applications.

One of the primary uses of UIManager is to set global properties that affect the overall appearance of Swing components throughout the application. This includes properties such as fonts, colors, borders, and default rendering styles. Developers can modify these properties using the put() method of the UIManager class, which allows them to specify key-value pairs for different UI defaults. For example, to change the default font used by all Swing components in an application, developers can use the following command:

javaCopy code

```java
UIManager.put("Label.font", new Font("Arial", Font.PLAIN, 12));
```

This command sets the default font for JLabel components to Arial with a plain style and a size of 12 points. Similarly, developers can customize other properties such as colors, borders, and rendering styles by specifying the appropriate keys and values in the UIManager.

In addition to setting individual properties, developers can install custom look and feel themes to completely change the appearance of their Swing applications. Look and feel themes define the visual style of UI components, including their colors, fonts, icons, and layout styles. Swing provides several built-in look and feel themes, such as Metal, Nimbus, and Windows, but developers can also create and install custom themes to achieve unique and branded designs.

To install a custom look and feel theme, developers typically need to include the theme's JAR file in their application's classpath and then set the UIManager's "lookAndFeel" property to the fully qualified class name of the theme's UIManager subclass. For example, to install the "Acme" look and feel theme, developers can use the following command:

javaCopy code

```
UIManager.setLookAndFeel("com.acme.ui.AcmeLookAndFeel");
```

This command sets the look and feel of the application to the custom "AcmeLookAndFeel" class, which is responsible for defining the visual style of the UI components according to the Acme theme.

Furthermore, developers can customize specific aspects of the installed look and feel theme by setting UIManager properties to override default values. For example, they can change the background color of all buttons in the application by using the following command:

javaCopy code

```java
UIManager.put( "Button.background" , Color.RED);
```

This command sets the background color of all JButton components to red, overriding the default value defined by the installed look and feel theme.

Another advanced technique for customizing UI components with UIManager is to create custom UI delegates for specific Swing components. UI delegates are responsible for rendering the visual representation of UI components, and developers can create custom delegates to implement custom rendering logic or to enhance the default behavior of Swing components. Custom UI delegates are typically subclasses of existing UI delegate classes, and they can be installed globally using the UIManager or set specifically for individual components using the setUI() method. For example, developers can create a custom UI delegate for JButton components to change their default appearance and behavior:

javaCopy code

```java
public class CustomButtonUI extends BasicButtonUI { @Override public void installUI(JComponent c) { super.installUI(c); AbstractButton button = (AbstractButton) c; button.setBackground(Color.YELLOW); } }
```

In this example, a custom UI delegate named CustomButtonUI is created by subclassing BasicButtonUI, the default UI delegate for JButton components. The installUI() method is overridden to customize the appearance of the button by setting its background color to yellow.

Once the custom UI delegate is defined, developers can install it globally for all JButton components in the application using the following command:

javaCopy code

```
UIManager.put( "ButtonUI",
"com.example.ui.CustomButtonUI" );
```

This command sets the default UI delegate for all JButton components to the custom CustomButtonUI class, ensuring that all buttons in the application use the custom appearance and behavior defined by the UI delegate.

In summary, customizing UI components with UIManager is a powerful technique for Java Swing developers to create visually appealing and branded user interfaces for their applications. By setting global properties, installing custom look and feel themes, and creating custom UI delegates, developers can achieve a high degree of customization and control over the appearance and behavior of Swing components, allowing them to create UIs that meet specific design requirements and provide an enhanced user experience. Whether it's adjusting fonts and colors, installing custom themes, or creating custom rendering logic, UIManager provides developers with the flexibility and versatility they need to create polished and professional Swing applications.

Implementing custom themes is a pivotal aspect of user

interface (UI) development, allowing developers to tailor the visual appearance of applications to match branding requirements, user preferences, or specific design aesthetics. In Java Swing applications, custom themes offer a way to override the default look and feel (L&F) provided by the platform and create a unique visual identity for the application. Leveraging custom themes empowers developers to create cohesive, visually appealing interfaces that resonate with users and reinforce brand identity.

A fundamental approach to implementing custom themes in Swing applications involves utilizing the built-in UIManager class, which serves as a central repository for managing UI-related properties and configurations. By modifying UIManager properties, developers can customize various aspects of the application's appearance, including colors, fonts, borders, and rendering styles. This allows for comprehensive theming capabilities without the need for extensive code changes or modifications to individual UI components.

To implement a custom theme using the UIManager, developers start by defining a set of key-value pairs that represent the desired visual properties of the application. These properties can include colors, fonts, and other UI-related attributes. Once the theme properties are defined, developers use the UIManager's put() method to assign these properties to specific keys, effectively customizing the appearance of Swing components throughout the application.

For instance, to create a custom theme with a specific color scheme, developers can set the background and foreground colors for various UI components using the following commands:

javaCopy code

```java
UIManager.put("Panel.background", Color.WHITE);
UIManager.put("Panel.foreground", Color.BLACK);
UIManager.put("Button.background", Color.BLUE);
UIManager.put("Button.foreground", Color.WHITE);
```

In this example, the background and foreground colors for JPanel and JButton components are defined to create a consistent color scheme across the application. By specifying these properties in the UIManager, developers ensure that all instances of these components adhere to the custom theme's color scheme.

Additionally, developers can define custom fonts and font sizes to further enhance the theme's visual appeal and readability. For example, to set a custom font for all JLabel components in the application, developers can use the following command:

javaCopy code

```java
UIManager.put("Label.font", new Font("Arial", Font.BOLD, 14));
```

This command specifies the Arial font with bold styling and a font size of 14 points for all JLabel components, ensuring a consistent and visually appealing typography throughout the application.

In addition to modifying individual properties, developers can apply custom look and feel (L&F) themes to completely transform the visual appearance of the application. Custom L&F themes provide a comprehensive set of visual styles and components that override the default Swing L&F, allowing developers to create unique and cohesive UI designs.

Implementing a custom L&F theme typically involves creating a custom subclass of a Swing L&F class, such as BasicLookAndFeel or SynthLookAndFeel, and overriding its methods to define the visual styles and components. Once the custom L&F theme is implemented, developers can install it in the application using the UIManager's setLookAndFeel() method.

For example, to apply a custom L&F theme named "MyCustomLookAndFeel" to the application, developers can use the following command:

javaCopy code

```
UIManager.setLookAndFeel("com.example.MyCustomL
ookAndFeel");
```

This command instructs the UIManager to use the custom L&F theme provided by the "MyCustomLookAndFeel" class, effectively applying the theme's visual styles and components to the entire application.

Furthermore, developers can package custom themes as external resources, such as JAR files, to facilitate theme reuse and distribution across multiple applications. By packaging custom themes as standalone resources, developers can easily apply them to different projects without duplicating code or configurations.

In summary, implementing custom themes is a crucial aspect of UI development in Java Swing applications, enabling developers to create visually stunning and cohesive user interfaces that align with branding requirements and design aesthetics. By leveraging the UIManager and custom L&F themes, developers can customize various aspects of the application's appearance, including colors, fonts, and visual styles, to create unique and memorable user experiences. Whether it's defining custom properties in the UIManager or implementing custom L&F themes, custom theming offers a flexible and powerful mechanism for creating polished and professional UI designs in Swing applications.

## Chapter 3: Advanced Layout Management

Exploring GroupLayout for complex layouts in Java Swing applications is an essential endeavor for developers seeking precise control and flexibility over their user interface designs. GroupLayout, introduced in Java SE 6, offers a powerful layout manager that enables developers to create sophisticated and intricate layouts with ease. Unlike other layout managers, GroupLayout allows developers to define the exact positioning and alignment of components, making it ideal for building complex and pixel-perfect user interfaces.

To utilize GroupLayout effectively, developers must understand its fundamental concepts and usage patterns. GroupLayout organizes components into horizontal and vertical groups, which dictate their arrangement along the X and Y axes, respectively. These groups can contain individual components, nested groups, or gaps, providing developers with fine-grained control over the layout structure. By nesting groups within groups, developers can create hierarchical layouts that accommodate various design requirements and adapt to different screen sizes and resolutions.

Creating a GroupLayout layout involves defining horizontal and vertical group sequences that specify the arrangement of components within the layout container. Developers typically use the GroupLayout.createParallelGroup() and GroupLayout.createSequentialGroup() methods to create horizontal and vertical groups, respectively. These methods allow developers to add components or other groups to the layout sequentially, specifying their alignment and sizing constraints as needed.

For example, to create a horizontal group that aligns components along the baseline, developers can use the following commands:

javaCopy code

```
GroupLayout.Group horizontalGroup = layout.createParallelGroup(GroupLayout.Alignment.BASELINE); horizontalGroup.addComponent(label1); horizontalGroup.addComponent(label2);
```

In this example, a horizontal group is created using the GroupLayout.createParallelGroup() method, and components label1 and label2 are added to the group. By specifying GroupLayout.Alignment.BASELINE, the components are aligned along their baseline, ensuring consistent vertical alignment across the layout.

Similarly, developers can create vertical groups using the GroupLayout.createSequentialGroup() method and add components or groups to the layout vertically:

javaCopy code

```
GroupLayout.Group verticalGroup = layout.createSequentialGroup();
verticalGroup.addComponent(label1);
verticalGroup.addComponent(label2);
```

By adding components or groups to both horizontal and vertical sequences, developers can construct complex layouts that accommodate various design requirements and adapt to different screen sizes and resolutions. Additionally, GroupLayout supports features such as component resizing, component hiding, and automatic gap insertion, allowing developers to create dynamic and responsive user interfaces.

An essential aspect of exploring GroupLayout is mastering its advanced features and techniques for handling complex layout scenarios. GroupLayout offers several advanced features, such as component alignment, resizing behavior, and baseline alignment, that enable developers to achieve precise control over component placement and sizing. For example, developers can use the GroupLayout.Alignment enumeration to specify how components should be aligned within their groups, such as leading, trailing, baseline, or center alignment.

javaCopy code

```
horizontalGroup.addGroup(layout.createSequentialGroup() .addComponent(label1) .addComponent(label2, GroupLayout.DEFAULT_SIZE, GroupLayout.DEFAULT_SIZE, GroupLayout.PREFERRED_SIZE));
```

In this example, label1 is aligned to the leading edge of the group, while label2 is aligned to the trailing edge with preferred sizing constraints. By leveraging alignment options and sizing constraints, developers can create layouts that adapt to different screen sizes and orientations while maintaining consistent component placement and alignment.

Furthermore, GroupLayout supports component resizing behavior, allowing developers to specify how components should resize when the container's size changes. Developers can use the GroupLayout.setHorizontalGroup() and GroupLayout.setVerticalGroup() methods to define resizing behavior for horizontal and vertical groups, respectively. By specifying resizing constraints such as minimum, preferred, and maximum sizes, developers can ensure that components resize appropriately to accommodate changes in the container's size.

javaCopy code

```
horizontalGroup.addComponent(label1)
.addPreferredGap(LayoutStyle.ComponentPlacement.UN
RELATED) .addComponent(label2);
```

In this example, a predefined gap of fixed size is inserted between label1 and label2 using the LayoutStyle.ComponentPlacement enumeration. By inserting gaps between components, developers can create visually appealing spacing and alignment within their layouts, enhancing readability and aesthetics.

Exploring GroupLayout for complex layouts also involves understanding how to handle nested and aligned groups effectively. GroupLayout supports nested groups, allowing developers to create hierarchical layouts with multiple levels of nesting. By nesting groups within groups, developers can organize components into logical units and apply alignment and sizing constraints at different levels of the layout hierarchy.

javaCopy code

```
horizontalGroup.addGroup(layout.createParallelGroup()
.addComponent(label1)
.addGroup(layout.createSequentialGroup()
.addComponent(label2) .addComponent(label3)));
```

In this example, label1 is added to the horizontal group directly, while label2 and label3 are nested within a nested group. By nesting components within groups, developers can achieve complex layout structures that adapt to different screen sizes and orientations while maintaining consistent alignment and spacing.

In summary, exploring GroupLayout for complex layouts in Java Swing applications is an essential skill for developers seeking precise control and flexibility over their user interface designs. By mastering GroupLayout's fundamental concepts, advanced features, and usage patterns, developers can create sophisticated and visually appealing layouts that adapt to different screen sizes and resolutions. Whether it's aligning components along baselines, specifying resizing behavior, or handling nested groups effectively, GroupLayout offers a powerful and versatile layout manager for building complex and pixel-perfect user interfaces in Java Swing applications.

Achieving fine-grained control with GridBagLayout in Java Swing applications is a fundamental skill that empowers developers to create complex and precisely arranged user interfaces. GridBagLayout offers a flexible and powerful layout manager that allows developers to create sophisticated layouts by arranging components into rows and columns using a grid-based system. Unlike other layout managers, GridBagLayout provides fine-grained control over the placement, sizing, and alignment of components within the layout, enabling developers to create pixel-perfect designs that adapt to different screen sizes and resolutions.
To utilize GridBagLayout effectively, developers must understand its core concepts and usage patterns. At the heart of GridBagLayout is the GridBagConstraints class, which encapsulates the constraints applied to each component within the layout. These constraints specify parameters such as grid position, alignment, padding, and resizing behavior, allowing developers to precisely control

the placement and appearance of components within the layout grid.

Creating a GridBagLayout layout involves defining GridBagConstraints for each component and adding them to the layout container using the layout's addComponent() method. Developers typically create GridBagConstraints instances by instantiating the class and setting its properties according to the desired layout constraints.

For example, to create a GridBagLayout layout with a JLabel positioned at row 0, column 0, developers can use the following commands:

javaCopy code

```
GridBagConstraints constraints = new GridBagConstraints(); constraints.gridx = 0; constraints.gridy = 0; container.add(label, constraints);
```

In this example, a GridBagConstraints instance is created, and its gridx and gridy properties are set to 0 to specify the component's position in the layout grid. The JLabel component is then added to the layout container using the specified constraints, ensuring that it appears at the specified grid position.

GridBagLayout also supports advanced features such as component spanning, which allows developers to merge multiple grid cells to accommodate larger components or create complex layout structures. By setting the gridwidth and gridheight properties of GridBagConstraints, developers can specify the number of cells that a component occupies within the layout grid.

For example, to create a JLabel that spans two columns in a GridBagLayout layout, developers can use the following commands:

javaCopy code

```
GridBagConstraints constraints = new GridBagConstraints(); constraints.gridx = 0; constraints.gridy = 0; constraints.gridwidth = 2; container.add(label, constraints);
```

In this example, the gridwidth property of GridBagConstraints is set to 2, indicating that the JLabel component should span two columns within the layout grid. This allows developers to create more complex and visually appealing layouts by combining multiple components into larger units.

Another essential aspect of achieving fine-grained control with GridBagLayout is understanding how to customize layout constraints to achieve specific design goals. GridBagConstraints offers a wide range of properties that developers can adjust to control component placement, alignment, padding, and resizing behavior.

For example, developers can use the anchor property of GridBagConstraints to specify how a component should be aligned within its cell. By default, components are centered within their cells, but developers can change this behavior by setting the anchor property to values such as GridBagConstraints.NORTH, GridBagConstraints.SOUTH, GridBagConstraints.EAST, or GridBagConstraints.WEST to align components to different sides of their cells.

javaCopy code

```
GridBagConstraints constraints = new GridBagConstraints(); constraints.gridx = 0; constraints.gridy = 0; constraints.anchor = GridBagConstraints.WEST; container.add(label, constraints);
```

In this example, the anchor property of GridBagConstraints is set to GridBagConstraints.WEST, causing the JLabel component to be aligned to the left side of its cell within the layout grid. This allows developers to achieve precise alignment and positioning of components within their layouts, ensuring a visually consistent and aesthetically pleasing user interface.

Furthermore, GridBagLayout supports component padding and insets, allowing developers to add spacing around components to improve readability and aesthetics. By adjusting the insets property of GridBagConstraints, developers can add padding around components to create a visually appealing spacing between adjacent components.

javaCopy code

```java
GridBagConstraints constraints = new GridBagConstraints(); constraints.gridx = 0; constraints.gridy = 0; constraints.insets = new Insets(5, 5, 5, 5); container.add(label, constraints);
```

In this example, the insets property of GridBagConstraints is set to create a padding of 5 pixels on all sides of the JLabel component within the layout grid. This adds spacing around the component, enhancing its visual appearance and improving readability within the layout.

Achieving fine-grained control with GridBagLayout also involves understanding how to handle component resizing and responsiveness within the layout. GridBagConstraints offers properties such as fill and weightx/weighty, which allow developers to control how components resize and distribute extra space within the layout grid.

For example, developers can use the fill property of GridBagConstraints to specify how a component should resize to fill its cell within the layout grid. By default, components are resized to fill their cells horizontally and vertically, but developers can change this behavior by setting the fill property to values such as GridBagConstraints.HORIZONTAL, GridBagConstraints.VERTICAL, or GridBagConstraints.BOTH to control the resizing behavior along different axes.

javaCopy code

```
GridBagConstraints constraints = new GridBagConstraints(); constraints.gridx = 0; constraints.gridy = 0; constraints.fill = GridBagConstraints.HORIZONTAL; container.add(label, constraints);
```

In this example, the fill property of GridBagConstraints is set to GridBagConstraints.HORIZONTAL, causing the JLabel component to resize horizontally to fill its cell within the layout grid. This allows developers to create responsive and adaptable layouts that adjust dynamically to changes in the container's size or content.

Additionally, developers can use the weightx and weighty properties of GridBagConstraints to control how extra space is distributed among components within the layout grid. By default, components are allocated equal amounts of extra space when the container is resized, but developers can adjust the weightx and weighty properties to specify how much extra space each component should receive relative to others.

javaCopy code

```
GridBagConstraints constraints = new GridBagConstraints(); constraints.gridx = 0;
```

```
constraints.gridy = 0; constraints.weightx = 1.0;
constraints.weighty = 1.0; container.add(label,
constraints);
```

In this example, the weightx and weighty properties of GridBagConstraints are set to 1.0, indicating that the JLabel component should receive a higher priority for extra space allocation within the layout grid.

## Chapter 4: Implementing Drag-and-Drop Functionality

Drag-and-drop functionality within the same application is a significant feature that enhances user experience and enables intuitive interaction in Java Swing applications. This capability allows users to effortlessly rearrange items, such as components or data, within the application's interface by dragging them from one location to another. Implementing drag-and-drop functionality within the same application involves several steps, including setting up drag and drop handlers, defining drag sources and drop targets, and handling drag-and-drop events.

To implement drag-and-drop functionality within the same application, developers utilize classes and interfaces provided by the Java Swing API, such as TransferHandler, DragSource, and DropTarget. These classes facilitate the management of drag-and-drop operations, including initiating drags, handling drag events, and processing drops.

The first step in enabling drag-and-drop functionality within the same application is to define drag sources, which are components or elements from which users can initiate drag operations. Developers typically attach a TransferHandler to drag source components to enable drag gesture recognition and provide data to be transferred during drag operations.

For example, to enable drag-and-drop functionality for a JPanel component, developers can set its

TransferHandler to a custom TransferHandler implementation:

javaCopy code

```
JPanel panel = new JPanel();
panel.setTransferHandler(new MyTransferHandler());
```

In this example, MyTransferHandler is a custom TransferHandler subclass that defines the behavior of drag-and-drop operations for the JPanel component.

Next, developers need to define drop targets, which are components or areas where users can drop dragged items. Drop targets must implement the DropTargetListener interface to handle drop events and process dropped data.

For instance, to define a drop target for another JPanel component, developers can create a custom DropTargetListener implementation:

javaCopy code

```
JPanel dropTarget = new JPanel();
dropTarget.setDropTarget(new
DropTarget(dropTarget, new
MyDropTargetListener()));
```

In this example, MyDropTargetListener is a custom implementation of the DropTargetListener interface that defines the behavior of drop operations for the dropTarget JPanel component.

Once drag sources and drop targets are defined, developers need to handle drag-and-drop events to facilitate data transfer between components. This involves implementing methods to respond to drag initiation, drag over, drag exit, and drop events.

For example, in the custom TransferHandler implementation for drag sources, developers override methods such as exportAsDrag() to initiate drag operations and exportDone() to handle the completion of drag operations:

javaCopy code

```
public class MyTransferHandler extends TransferHandler { @Override protected void exportAsDrag(JComponent comp, InputEvent e, int action) { // Perform custom drag initialization } @Override protected void exportDone(JComponent source, Transferable data, int action) { // Perform custom drag completion handling } }
```

Similarly, in the custom DropTargetListener implementation for drop targets, developers override methods such as dragEnter() to handle drag entering the drop target area and drop() to process dropped data:

javaCopy code

```
public class MyDropTargetListener implements DropTargetListener { @Override public void dragEnter(DropTargetDragEvent dtde) { // Handle drag entering the drop target area } @Override public void drop(DropTargetDropEvent dtde) { // Handle data transfer on drop } }
```

These methods allow developers to customize the behavior of drag-and-drop operations and define how data is transferred between drag sources and drop targets within the same application.

In addition to handling drag-and-drop events, developers may also need to manage data transfer between drag sources and drop targets. This involves creating and configuring Transferable objects to encapsulate data being transferred during drag-and-drop operations.

For example, in the exportAsDrag() method of the custom TransferHandler implementation, developers can create a Transferable object containing the data to be transferred:

javaCopy code

```
@Override protected void exportAsDrag(JComponent comp, InputEvent e, int action) { Transferable transferable = new StringSelection("Dragged Data"); super.exportAsDrag(comp, e, action); }
```

In this example, a Transferable object is created using StringSelection to encapsulate a string representing the data being dragged. This Transferable object is then passed to the superclass method to initiate the drag operation.

Overall, implementing drag-and-drop functionality within the same application in Java Swing involves defining drag sources and drop targets, handling drag-and-drop events, and managing data transfer between components. By utilizing classes and interfaces provided by the Java Swing API, developers can create intuitive and interactive user interfaces that enable seamless rearrangement of items within the application's interface.

Drag-and-drop functionality between different

applications is a valuable feature that enhances user productivity and facilitates seamless data exchange in modern graphical user interfaces. Enabling drag-and-drop between different applications allows users to transfer data, such as files, text, or images, between disparate software tools with ease. Implementing drag-and-drop between different applications involves utilizing platform-specific mechanisms, such as data transfer protocols and interprocess communication, to facilitate the transfer of data across application boundaries.

To enable drag-and-drop between different applications, developers leverage platform-specific APIs and technologies that support inter-application communication and data exchange. On desktop operating systems such as Windows, macOS, and Linux, developers typically rely on platform APIs, such as the Windows API, AppleScript, or the X Window System, to implement drag-and-drop functionality between applications.

One approach to enabling drag-and-drop between different applications is to use the clipboard as an intermediary for data transfer. In this approach, when a user initiates a drag operation in one application, the selected data is copied to the clipboard in a format that can be understood by both the source and destination applications. The destination application then retrieves the data from the clipboard and processes it accordingly.

For example, on Windows, developers can use the Win32 API functions, such as OpenClipboard,

SetClipboardData, and CloseClipboard, to interact with the clipboard and transfer data between applications programmatically. Similarly, on macOS, developers can use the NSPasteboard class in Cocoa to access the system clipboard and exchange data between applications.

Another approach to enabling drag-and-drop between different applications is to use platform-specific drag-and-drop protocols and mechanisms. Many modern desktop environments provide support for drag-and-drop operations between applications using standardized protocols and APIs.

For instance, on macOS, developers can leverage the Apple Event Manager and the Drag Manager APIs to implement drag-and-drop functionality between Cocoa applications. Similarly, on Linux systems running the X Window System, developers can use the Xdnd (X Drag-and-Drop) protocol to enable drag-and-drop between X11 applications.

One common technique for enabling drag-and-drop between different applications is to implement support for standard data formats and MIME types that are widely supported across platforms. By using standard data formats such as plain text, HTML, or images, developers can ensure compatibility with a wide range of applications and environments.

For example, when implementing drag-and-drop between a text editor and a web browser, developers can use plain text or HTML as the data format for transferring text content. This allows users to drag text snippets from the editor and drop them into text fields or text areas within the web browser, facilitating seamless data exchange between the two applications.

Furthermore, developers can implement support for custom data formats and MIME types to enable more sophisticated drag-and-drop scenarios between different applications. By defining custom data formats and serialization mechanisms, developers can transfer complex data structures and objects between applications using drag-and-drop.

For instance, when implementing drag-and-drop between a graphics editor and a presentation software, developers can define a custom data format for transferring image data along with metadata such as dimensions, color depth, and file format. This allows users to drag images from the graphics editor and drop them directly into slide placeholders within the presentation software, streamlining the workflow for creating multimedia presentations.

In addition to implementing drag-and-drop functionality within their applications, developers must also handle drag-and-drop events and data processing on the receiving end. When a drop event occurs in the destination application, developers must extract the transferred data from the drag event and process it accordingly.

For example, when implementing drag-and-drop between a file manager and an image viewer, developers must handle drop events in the image viewer application and extract the file paths or image data from the drag event. They can then load the dropped files or images into the viewer's display area for viewing and manipulation.

Overall, enabling drag-and-drop between different applications involves leveraging platform-specific APIs, data transfer protocols, and interprocess communication mechanisms to facilitate seamless data exchange across application boundaries. By implementing support for standard data formats, custom data formats, and drag-and-drop protocols, developers can empower users to transfer data between disparate software tools with ease, enhancing productivity and usability in graphical user interfaces.

## Chapter 5: Enhancing User Experience with Tooltips and Cursors

Customizing tooltips for component information is a crucial aspect of enhancing user experience and providing informative guidance within Java Swing applications. Tooltips serve as brief informational messages that appear when users hover over user interface components such as buttons, labels, or text fields, offering contextual insights or instructions regarding the component's functionality. Customizing tooltips allows developers to tailor the information presented to users, providing relevant details that aid in understanding and navigating the application's interface effectively.

In Java Swing applications, customizing tooltips involves defining custom tooltip text for individual components and customizing the appearance and behavior of tooltips to suit the application's requirements. The javax.swing.ToolTipManager class provides the primary mechanism for customizing tooltips in Swing applications, allowing developers to set the default tooltip delay, enable or disable tooltips, and customize the tooltip generation process.

To customize tooltips for specific components in a Java Swing application, developers typically use the setToolTipText() method provided by Swing components to set custom tooltip text. This method allows developers to specify the text that should be displayed when users hover over the component with the mouse cursor.

For example, to set a custom tooltip for a JButton component, developers can use the setToolTipText() method to specify the tooltip text:

javaCopy code

```
JButton button = new JButton("Click Me");
button.setToolTipText("This is a custom tooltip for the button");
```

In this example, the tooltip text "This is a custom tooltip for the button" will be displayed when users hover over the JButton component with the mouse cursor.

Furthermore, developers can customize the appearance and behavior of tooltips using the UIManager class and Look and Feel settings provided by Swing. UIManager allows developers to set global properties for Swing components, including tooltip background color, foreground color, font, and border.

For instance, to customize the background color of tooltips in a Java Swing application, developers can use the put() method of the UIManager class to set the "ToolTip.background" property:

javaCopy code

```
UIManager.put("ToolTip.background", Color.YELLOW);
```

In this example, tooltips in the application will have a yellow background color when displayed.

Additionally, developers can customize tooltip behavior by adjusting the tooltip display delay and dismissal delay using the setInitialDelay() and setDismissDelay() methods of the ToolTipManager class, respectively.

These methods allow developers to control the timing of tooltip display and dismissal, ensuring that tooltips appear and disappear at appropriate times.

javaCopy code

```
ToolTipManager.sharedInstance().setInitialDelay( 500 );
ToolTipManager.sharedInstance().setDismissDelay( 200
0 );
```

In this example, tooltips will appear after a delay of 500 milliseconds and disappear after a delay of 2000 milliseconds when users hover over components with the mouse cursor.

Moreover, developers can create custom tooltip components using the JToolTip class to provide more complex or interactive tooltip content. By subclassing JToolTip and overriding its paintComponent() method, developers can create custom tooltip designs and incorporate interactive elements such as buttons or hyperlinks.

javaCopy code

```
public class CustomToolTip extends JToolTip {
@Override protected void paintComponent(Graphics
g) { // Custom tooltip painting logic } }
```

In this example, developers can implement custom painting logic within the paintComponent() method to create a unique visual style for tooltips.

Furthermore, developers can enhance tooltip usability by incorporating dynamic tooltip content that adapts to user interactions or application state changes. For example, developers can update tooltip text dynamically based on user input or display additional information when certain conditions are met.

javaCopy code

```
button.addMouseListener(new MouseAdapter() { @Override public void mouseEntered(MouseEvent e) { button.setToolTipText("Click this button to perform an action"); } });
```

In this example, the tooltip text for the JButton component is updated dynamically when users hover over the button with the mouse cursor.

Overall, customizing tooltips for component information in Java Swing applications involves setting custom tooltip text for individual components, adjusting tooltip appearance and behavior using UIManager and ToolTipManager settings, creating custom tooltip components, and incorporating dynamic tooltip content. By customizing tooltips effectively, developers can provide users with informative guidance and improve the usability and accessibility of their applications.

Changing cursor appearance for user feedback is an essential aspect of user interface design aimed at enhancing user experience and providing visual cues to indicate different states or actions within an application. In Java Swing applications, the cursor is a graphical representation of the user's interaction with the interface, and altering its appearance can effectively convey information about the current context or available actions. Customizing cursor appearance involves modifying the default cursor image or setting specific cursor shapes for different components or interaction events, enabling developers to provide meaningful feedback to users during various interactions.

In Java Swing applications, developers can customize cursor appearance using the java.awt.Cursor class, which provides methods for creating and manipulating cursor objects. By creating instances of the Cursor class with desired attributes, such as shape, size, and image, developers can change the appearance of the cursor to suit different application scenarios.

To change the cursor appearance in a Java Swing application, developers can create custom cursor objects using predefined cursor types or by loading custom cursor images. The Toolkit class provides methods for accessing system-defined cursor objects, such as default cursors for common interaction events like pointing, resizing, or text selection. Developers can use these predefined cursor types directly or customize them further by adjusting their appearance properties.

javaCopy code

```java
Cursor customCursor = Cursor.getPredefinedCursor(Cursor.HAND_CURSOR);
```

In this example, a custom cursor object is created using the predefined hand cursor type, which typically indicates clickable or interactive elements within an application. This custom cursor can then be assigned to specific components or interaction events to provide visual feedback to users.

Alternatively, developers can create custom cursor objects using custom cursor images loaded from external image files. This approach allows developers to create unique cursor designs that match the application's visual style or branding. To load a custom cursor image, developers can use the Toolkit class to create a cursor object from an Image object representing the cursor image.

javaCopy code

```
Image customCursorImage = Toolkit.getDefaultToolkit().getImage( "custom_cursor.png" ); Cursor customCursor = Toolkit.getDefaultToolkit().createCustomCursor(customCursorImage, new Point(0, 0), "custom_cursor" );
```

In this example, a custom cursor image named "custom_cursor.png" is loaded from an external file, and a custom cursor object is created using the loaded image. The cursor object's hotspot position is specified as (0, 0), indicating the cursor's reference point relative to its image, and a unique name ("custom_cursor") is assigned to the cursor object for identification purposes.

Once custom cursor objects are created, developers can assign them to specific Swing components or user interaction events using the setCursor() method provided by the Component class. By setting the cursor for individual components, developers can customize cursor appearance based on the component's role or function within the application.

javaCopy code

```
component.setCursor(customCursor);
```

In this example, the custom cursor object "customCursor" is assigned to the Swing component "component," causing the component's cursor to change to the custom cursor when users interact with it.

Moreover, developers can dynamically change cursor appearance in response to user actions or application state changes to provide real-time feedback to users. For example, developers can change cursor appearance to indicate loading or processing operations, hover effects over clickable elements, or drag-and-drop operations.

javaCopy code

```
component.addMouseListener( new MouseAdapter() { @Override public void mouseEntered(MouseEvent e) { component.setCursor(customCursor); } @Override public void mouseExited(MouseEvent e) { component.setCursor(Cursor.getDefaultCursor()); } });
```

In this example, the custom cursor "customCursor" is assigned to the Swing component "component" when users hover over it with the mouse cursor, providing visual feedback that the component is clickable or interactive. When users exit the component's bounds, the default cursor is restored using the getDefaultCursor() method of the Cursor class.

Furthermore, developers can utilize cursor appearance changes to convey specific meanings or instructions to users during different application states or interactions. By associating different cursor shapes or images with distinct actions or states, developers can guide users through the application's interface and improve usability and accessibility.

Overall, changing cursor appearance for user feedback in Java Swing applications involves creating custom cursor objects using predefined cursor types or custom cursor images, assigning custom cursors to specific components or interaction events, and dynamically changing cursor appearance to provide real-time feedback to users. By customizing cursor appearance effectively, developers can enhance user experience, convey meaningful information, and improve usability in their Swing applications.

## Chapter 6: Working with Icons and Images

Loading and displaying image icons is a fundamental aspect of graphical user interface (GUI) development, crucial for creating visually appealing and informative Java Swing applications. Icons serve various purposes within an application, including representing buttons, menu items, toolbar elements, or indicating application state and status. In Java Swing, developers can load and display image icons using different approaches, including loading images from local files, resources bundled within the application JAR file, or downloading images from remote sources. These icons can then be integrated into Swing components to enhance the application's visual presentation and provide intuitive user interaction.

One common approach to loading and displaying image icons in Java Swing applications is to load images from local files stored on the file system. This approach allows developers to use image editing tools to create custom icons in various formats, such as PNG, JPEG, or GIF, and then load them directly into Swing components.

To load and display an image icon from a local file in a Java Swing application, developers can use the ImageIcon class provided by Swing, which simplifies the process of loading and managing image resources. The ImageIcon class allows developers to create ImageIcon objects from image files and then assign them to Swing components such as JLabels, JButtons, or JMenuItem objects.

javaCopy code

```
ImageIcon icon = new ImageIcon("path/to/image.png"); JLabel label = new JLabel(icon);
```

In this example, an ImageIcon object is created by specifying the file path to the image file "image.png". The ImageIcon object is then assigned to a JLabel component, which displays the image icon within the application's user interface.

Another approach to loading and displaying image icons in Java Swing applications is to embed image resources directly within the application JAR file. This approach ensures that the application has access to its required image resources regardless of the deployment environment and simplifies distribution by bundling all required resources within a single JAR file.

To embed image resources within a Java Swing application JAR file, developers typically create a dedicated "resources" directory within the project directory structure and place image files inside this directory. During the build process, the build tool (e.g., Apache Maven or Gradle) includes these image resources in the generated JAR file, allowing the application to access them at runtime.

plaintextCopy code

```
project | src | └── main | ├── java | └── resources | └── image.png
```

Once image resources are embedded within the JAR file, developers can load and display image icons using the ImageIcon class as before, specifying the resource path relative to the application's classpath.

javaCopy code

```
ImageIcon icon = new ImageIcon(getClass().getResource("/image.png"));
JLabel label = new JLabel(icon);
```

In this example, the getResource() method is used to retrieve the image resource "image.png" from the application's classpath. The ImageIcon object is then created using the retrieved resource URL, allowing the application to access the image icon regardless of its deployment location.

Additionally, developers can load and display image icons dynamically from remote sources such as URLs or web services, enabling applications to fetch and display image resources hosted on external servers or cloud storage platforms. This approach is useful for applications that require dynamic content or regularly updated image resources.

To load and display an image icon from a remote URL in a Java Swing application, developers can use the ImageIcon class in conjunction with the URL class to fetch image resources over the network.

javaCopy code

```
URL imageUrl = new URL("https://example.com/image.png"); ImageIcon icon = new ImageIcon(imageUrl); JLabel label = new JLabel(icon);
```

In this example, the URL class is used to create a URL object representing the remote image resource "https://example.com/image.png". The ImageIcon object is then created using the URL object, allowing the application to fetch and display the image icon from the specified URL.

Furthermore, developers can customize the appearance and behavior of image icons by scaling, resizing, or applying image processing effects using standard Java image manipulation APIs such as the java.awt.image package. These APIs provide functionality for performing various image operations, including scaling, cropping, rotating, and applying image filters or effects.

javaCopy code

```
ImageIcon icon = new ImageIcon("path/to/image.png"); Image scaledImage = icon.getImage().getScaledInstance(100, 100, Image.SCALE_SMOOTH); icon = new ImageIcon(scaledImage); JLabel label = new JLabel(icon);
```

In this example, the getImage() method is used to retrieve the image associated with the ImageIcon object. The getScaledInstance() method is then called to scale the image to the desired dimensions (100x100 pixels) with smooth scaling interpolation. Finally, the scaled image is used to create a new ImageIcon object, which is assigned to a JLabel component for display.

Overall, loading and displaying image icons in Java Swing applications is a versatile and essential technique for enhancing the visual presentation and usability of

GUIs. By leveraging the ImageIcon class and various image loading strategies, developers can incorporate custom icons into Swing components, providing users with intuitive visual cues and improving the overall user experience.

In Java Swing applications, loading and displaying image icons play a significant role in enhancing the visual appeal and usability of graphical user interfaces (GUIs). Developers often need to incorporate custom image icons from external files to represent various elements within the application, such as buttons, labels, or menu items. Creating custom image icons from files involves several steps, including loading image files from the filesystem, converting them into suitable formats for display, and integrating them into Swing components seamlessly.

The first step in creating custom image icons from files is to load the image files from the filesystem into the Java application. Java provides several classes and utilities for reading image files, such as BufferedImage, ImageIO, and ImageIcon. Developers can use these classes to load image files in popular formats like JPEG, PNG, or GIF.

To load an image file from the filesystem into a Java application, developers typically use the ImageIO class, which provides static methods for reading images from various sources, including files, URLs, and input streams. The following code demonstrates how to load an image file named "icon.png" from the filesystem:

javaCopy code

```
try { BufferedImage image = ImageIO.read(new File("icon.png")); } catch (IOException e) { e.printStackTrace(); }
```

In this example, the ImageIO.read() method is used to read the image file "icon.png" from the filesystem and load it into a BufferedImage object. If the image file is not found or an error occurs during loading, an IOException is thrown and handled accordingly.

Once the image file is loaded into memory as a BufferedImage object, developers can create ImageIcon objects to represent the image icons within the Swing components. ImageIcon is a Swing-specific class that wraps an Image object and provides additional functionality for displaying images within GUI components.

javaCopy code

```
ImageIcon icon = new ImageIcon("icon.png");
```

In this example, an ImageIcon object named "icon" is created using the image file "icon.png" loaded from the filesystem. The ImageIcon object can now be assigned to various Swing components, such as JLabels, JButtons, or JMenuItems, to display the corresponding image icon within the GUI.

To integrate the custom image icons into Swing components, developers can use setter methods provided by Swing components to assign ImageIcon objects as their icons. For example, to set an image icon for a JButton component, developers can use the setIcon() method as follows:

javaCopy code

JButton button = new JButton("Click Me"); button.setIcon(icon);

In this example, the ImageIcon object "icon" is assigned as the icon for the JButton component "button," causing the button to display the corresponding image icon alongside its text label.

Furthermore, developers can customize the appearance and behavior of image icons within Swing components by adjusting various properties, such as size, alignment, and scaling. ImageIcon provides methods for resizing and scaling image icons to fit different container sizes or aspect ratios.

javaCopy code

```
Image scaledImage = icon.getImage().getScaledInstance(50, 50, Image.SCALE_SMOOTH); Icon scaledIcon = new ImageIcon(scaledImage); button.setIcon(scaledIcon);
```

In this example, the getImage() method of the ImageIcon object "icon" is used to retrieve the underlying Image object, which is then scaled to a size of 50x50 pixels using the getScaledInstance() method. The scaled Image object is then wrapped in a new ImageIcon object "scaledIcon" and assigned as the icon for the JButton component "button."

Additionally, developers can handle user interactions with image icons within Swing components by attaching event listeners or action listeners to the corresponding components. For example, developers can add action listeners to JButton components to respond to button clicks and perform specific actions.

javaCopy code

```
button.addActionListener(e -> { // Perform action when the button is clicked });
```

In this example, a lambda expression is used to define the action to be performed when the JButton component "button" is clicked. Developers can implement custom logic within the lambda expression to handle the button click event and respond accordingly.

Overall, creating custom image icons from files in Java Swing applications involves loading image files from the filesystem, creating ImageIcon objects to represent the image icons, integrating the image icons into Swing components, and customizing their appearance and behavior as needed. By incorporating custom image icons into Swing GUIs, developers can enhance the visual appeal and usability of their applications, providing users with intuitive and engaging interfaces.

## Chapter 7: Animation and Transition Effects

Creating smooth animation effects with Timer is a fundamental technique in Java Swing programming, essential for building dynamic and visually appealing user interfaces. Animation enhances user experience by adding interactivity, feedback, and aesthetic appeal to applications, making them more engaging and intuitive. In Java Swing, animation effects can be achieved using the javax.swing.Timer class, which allows developers to schedule repetitive tasks at specified intervals, making it ideal for implementing animations that require regular updates.

To create smooth animation effects with Timer in Java Swing, developers typically follow a series of steps to set up the animation loop, update the graphical components, and handle user interactions seamlessly. The process begins by defining the animation logic, including the duration, frame rate, and graphical elements to be animated. Once the animation parameters are established, developers can initialize a Timer object to control the animation loop and update the graphical components at regular intervals.

javaCopy code

```
Timer timer = new Timer(delayInMillis, ActionListener);
```

In this command, **delayInMillis** represents the delay between animation frames in milliseconds, and **ActionListener** is an ActionListener implementation responsible for updating the graphical components during each animation cycle.

Next, developers register the ActionListener with the Timer object and implement the actionPerformed() method to define the animation logic. Inside the actionPerformed() method, developers update the graphical components according to the desired animation effect, such as moving objects, changing colors, or scaling images.

javaCopy code

```
timer.addActionListener(new ActionListener() { public void actionPerformed(ActionEvent e) { // Update graphical components for animation } });
```

Within the actionPerformed() method, developers can manipulate Swing components, repaint the GUI, and trigger revalidation to reflect the changes visually. By updating the component properties incrementally over multiple animation cycles, developers can create smooth and fluid animation effects that enhance the user interface's dynamism and responsiveness.

One common animation technique achieved with Timer is sprite animation, where a series of images representing different animation frames are displayed sequentially to create the illusion of motion. To implement sprite animation with Timer, developers load a sequence of images into memory and update the graphical component's image property at regular intervals to display each frame of the animation.

javaCopy code

```
BufferedImage[] frames = loadAnimationFrames(); int currentFrameIndex = 0; timer.addActionListener(new ActionListener() { public void actionPerformed(ActionEvent e) { // Update the image to display the current animation frame imageLabel.setIcon(new ImageIcon(frames[currentFrameIndex])); // Increment the frame index for the next animation cycle currentFrameIndex = (currentFrameIndex + 1) % frames.length; } });
```

In this example, **loadAnimationFrames()** is a custom method that loads an array of BufferedImage objects representing the animation frames. Within the actionPerformed() method, the image displayed by a JLabel component (**imageLabel**) is updated to the current animation frame, and the frame index is incremented to advance to the next frame in the sequence.

Additionally, developers can incorporate easing functions and interpolation techniques to create more realistic and visually appealing animation effects. Easing functions modify the rate of change of animation properties over time, allowing developers to simulate acceleration, deceleration, or other motion behaviors. By applying easing functions to animation parameters such as position, scale, and opacity, developers can achieve smoother transitions and more natural-looking animations.

javaCopy code

```
double progress = (double) elapsedTime / animationDuration; double easedProgress = easeInOut(progress); double interpolatedValue = startValue + (endValue - startValue) * easedProgress;
```

In this code snippet, **easeInOut()** is a custom easing function that modifies the progress value to achieve a smooth acceleration and deceleration effect. The interpolatedValue represents the interpolated animation property value calculated based on the eased progress, start value, and end value.

Furthermore, developers can optimize animation performance and reduce flickering by utilizing double buffering techniques and minimizing unnecessary repaints. Double buffering involves rendering animations off-screen in a separate buffer before displaying them on the screen, preventing visual artifacts such as tearing and flickering. By buffering animation frames and updating the display only when necessary, developers can ensure smoother animation playback and improve overall user experience.

javaCopy code

```
// Enable double buffering for smoother animation
JComponent.setDoubleBuffered( true );
```

In this command, **JComponent.setDoubleBuffered(true)** enables double buffering for the specified Swing component, ensuring that animation frames are rendered off-screen before being displayed to the user.

Overall, creating smooth animation effects with Timer in Java Swing involves defining the animation logic, updating graphical components at regular intervals, implementing sprite animation techniques, incorporating easing functions and interpolation, optimizing performance with double buffering, and fine-tuning animation parameters to achieve the desired visual effects. By leveraging Timer-based animation techniques effectively, developers can enhance the interactivity and visual appeal of Java Swing applications, providing users with engaging and immersive user experiences.

Implementing transition effects between Swing components is a pivotal aspect of user interface design, elevating the visual appeal and user experience of Java applications. Transition effects facilitate smooth and seamless transitions between different states or views within an application, enhancing the overall usability and engagement. In Java Swing, developers can implement transition effects using various techniques, including animation, opacity changes, and component resizing, to create visually compelling user interfaces that captivate and guide users through the application's workflow.

One effective technique for implementing transition effects between Swing components is leveraging animation to animate component properties, such as position, size, or opacity, over a specified duration. By animating these properties, developers can achieve smooth transitions between different UI states, providing users with visual cues that indicate changes in the application's state or navigation flow. To implement animation-based transition effects in Java Swing, developers typically use the javax.swing.Timer class to schedule animation updates and the java.awt.Graphics2D class to perform graphical transformations.

javaCopy code

```
Timer timer = new Timer(delayInMillis, new ActionListener() { @Override public void actionPerformed(ActionEvent e) { // Update animation state // Repaint component to reflect changes } });
```

In this command, **delayInMillis** represents the delay between animation frames in milliseconds, and the ActionListener is responsible for updating the animation state and repainting the component to reflect the changes visually. By scheduling animation updates at regular intervals, developers can create smooth and fluid transition effects that enhance the user interface's dynamism and responsiveness.

Another technique for implementing transition effects between Swing components is using opacity changes to fade components in or out during transitions. By adjusting the opacity property of Swing components gradually, developers can create fade-in or fade-out effects that smoothly blend components into or out of view, providing users with a visually pleasing transition between different UI states. To implement opacity-based transition effects, developers can use the java.awt.AlphaComposite class to adjust component opacity and the javax.swing.Timer class to schedule opacity updates over time.

javaCopy code

```
Timer timer = new Timer(delayInMillis, new ActionListener() { @Override public void actionPerformed(ActionEvent e) { // Update opacity property // Repaint component to reflect changes } });
```

In this command, the ActionListener updates the opacity property of the Swing component gradually over time, creating a fade-in or fade-out effect. By scheduling opacity updates at regular intervals, developers can achieve smooth and gradual transitions between different UI states, enhancing the overall user experience.

Additionally, developers can implement transition effects between Swing components by resizing or repositioning components dynamically to create sliding, scaling, or zooming effects. By animating component size or location changes, developers can create visually dynamic transitions that guide users' attention and provide context for changes in the application's state or layout. To implement size or position-based transition effects, developers can use the java.awt.Rectangle class to represent component bounds and the javax.swing.Timer class to schedule updates to component properties over time.

javaCopy code

```
Timer timer = new Timer(delayInMillis, new ActionListener() { @Override public void actionPerformed(ActionEvent e) { // Update component bounds // Repaint component to reflect changes } });
```

In this command, the ActionListener adjusts the component's bounds gradually over time, creating a smooth transition effect. By scheduling updates to component properties at regular intervals, developers can achieve fluid and dynamic transitions between different UI states, enhancing the overall user experience.

Moreover, developers can combine multiple transition techniques, such as animation, opacity changes, and component resizing, to create more complex and visually stunning transition effects in Java Swing applications. By experimenting with different transition techniques and parameters, developers can tailor transition effects to suit the application's visual style and user interface design, creating engaging and immersive user experiences that captivate and delight users.

In summary, implementing transition effects between Swing components is a powerful technique for enhancing the visual appeal and usability of Java applications. By leveraging animation, opacity changes, and component resizing, developers can create smooth and seamless transitions between different UI states, providing users with intuitive and engaging navigation experiences. With careful design and implementation, transition effects can elevate the overall quality of Java Swing applications, making them more attractive, user-friendly, and enjoyable to use.

## Chapter 8: Incorporating Multimedia Elements

Embedding audio clips in Swing applications is a valuable technique for enhancing user experience by adding sound effects, background music, or audio feedback to various interactions and events within the application. Audio clips can provide auditory cues that complement visual elements, improving accessibility, engagement, and immersion for users. In Java Swing, developers can integrate audio playback functionality using the javax.sound.sampled package, which provides classes and interfaces for loading, playing, and controlling audio clips programmatically. By incorporating audio clips into Swing applications, developers can create more dynamic and interactive user interfaces that appeal to a wider range of users and enhance the overall user experience.

To embed audio clips in Swing applications, developers first need to import the necessary classes and interfaces from the javax.sound.sampled package. This package provides a variety of classes for handling audio files, including Clip, AudioInputStream, and AudioSystem, which are essential for loading and playing audio clips programmatically.

javaCopy code

```
import javax.sound.sampled.*;
```

Once the necessary classes are imported, developers can load audio files into memory using the AudioSystem class's static methods. Audio files can be in various formats, such as WAV, MP3, or MIDI, but WAV files are commonly used for their simplicity and wide compatibility. To load an audio file into an AudioInputStream object, developers can use the AudioSystem.getAudioInputStream() method, passing a File or InputStream object representing the audio file.

javaCopy code

```java
AudioInputStream audioInputStream = AudioSystem.getAudioInputStream( new File( "audio_clip.wav" ));
```

In this command, "audio_clip.wav" is the filename of the audio file to be loaded into memory. Once the audio file is loaded into an AudioInputStream object, developers can create a Clip object to play the audio clip. The Clip interface represents a sound clip that can be loaded, played, paused, resumed, and stopped programmatically.

javaCopy code

```java
Clip clip = AudioSystem.getClip();
```

Next, developers need to open the Clip object and associate it with the loaded audio file using the open() method of the Clip interface. This method prepares the clip for playback and loads the audio data into memory, ready for playback.

javaCopy code

```java
clip.open(audioInputStream);
```

After the Clip object is opened and associated with the audio file, developers can play the audio clip using the start() method of the Clip interface. This method starts playback of the audio clip from the beginning.

javaCopy code

```
clip.start();
```

In this command, the start() method is called on the Clip object to initiate playback of the audio clip. Additionally, developers can control various aspects of audio playback, such as volume, balance, and looping, by setting properties of the Clip object before or during playback.

javaCopy code

```
clip.loop(Clip.LOOP_CONTINUOUSLY);
clip.setVolume(0.5f); clip.setBalance(0.0f);
```

In this example, the loop() method is called with the LOOP_CONTINUOUSLY constant to enable continuous looping of the audio clip. The setVolume() method adjusts the volume level of the audio clip, and the setBalance() method adjusts the balance between the left and right stereo channels. By adjusting these properties dynamically, developers can create more immersive and interactive audio experiences in Swing applications.

Furthermore, developers can handle various events and states of the Clip object, such as playback completion or errors, by registering event listeners with the Clip object. Event listeners can be implemented using the javax.sound.sampled.LineListener interface, which defines methods for handling line events, such as START, STOP, OPEN, and CLOSE.

javaCopy code

```
clip.addLineListener(new LineListener() { @Override
public void update(LineEvent event) { if
```

(event.getType() == LineEvent.Type.STOP) { // Handle playback completion } } });

In this example, an anonymous inner class is created to implement the LineListener interface, and the update() method is overridden to handle STOP events, indicating that playback of the audio clip has completed. By registering event listeners with the Clip object, developers can respond to various playback events and states, providing users with a more robust and reliable audio experience in Swing applications.

In summary, embedding audio clips in Swing applications is a powerful technique for enhancing user experience and engagement by adding sound effects, background music, or audio feedback to various interactions and events within the application. By leveraging the javax.sound.sampled package, developers can load, play, and control audio clips programmatically, enabling them to create more dynamic and immersive user interfaces that appeal to a wider audience. With careful design and implementation, audio clips can complement visual elements and enhance the overall user experience of Swing applications, making them more enjoyable, engaging, and memorable for users.

Displaying video content with JMF (Java Media Framework) is a powerful technique for enriching Java applications with multimedia capabilities, allowing developers to integrate video playback functionality seamlessly. JMF provides a robust and extensible platform for handling various multimedia formats, including video, audio, and streaming media, making it well-suited for creating interactive and immersive multimedia experiences. By leveraging JMF's comprehensive API and libraries, developers can load, decode, and render video content within Swing applications, providing users with compelling visual content and enhancing the overall user experience.

To display video content with JMF in a Swing application, developers first need to download and install the JMF library, which includes the necessary classes and libraries for multimedia processing. The JMF library can be downloaded from the Oracle website or other reputable sources and installed on the local system. Once installed, developers can include the JMF library in their Java project's classpath to access its functionality.

bashCopy code

```
javac -classpath jmf.jar YourJavaFile.java
```

In this command, "jmf.jar" represents the JMF library file, and "YourJavaFile.java" is the name of the Java source file containing the code for displaying video content. By including the JMF library in the classpath, developers ensure that their Java application can access the necessary JMF classes and libraries at runtime.

After including the JMF library in the classpath, developers can proceed to write code to display video content within a Swing application. To do this, developers typically use the javax.media package, which contains classes and interfaces for working with multimedia content in Java. One of the key classes provided by JMF for video playback is the Player interface, which represents a multimedia player capable of playing video, audio, or other multimedia content.

javaCopy code

```
import javax.media.*; import javax.swing.*; public class VideoPlayer extends JFrame { private Player player; public VideoPlayer(String videoFile) { try { MediaLocator mediaLocator = new MediaLocator("file:" + videoFile); player = Manager.createRealizedPlayer(mediaLocator); Component videoComponent = player.getVisualComponent(); add(videoComponent); player.start(); } catch (Exception e) { e.printStackTrace(); } } public static void main(String[] args) { SwingUtilities.invokeLater(() -> { new VideoPlayer("video_file.mp4").setVisible(true); }); } }
```

In this code example, a simple Swing application called "VideoPlayer" is created to display video content from a specified file. The constructor of the VideoPlayer class takes the path to the video file as a parameter and initializes a Player object to play the video. The Player object is created using the Manager.createRealizedPlayer() method, passing a MediaLocator object representing the location of the video file. The getVisualComponent() method of the Player interface returns a graphical component representing the video playback area, which is added to the JFrame using the add() method. Finally, the player is started using the start() method to begin video playback.

Once the VideoPlayer class is defined, developers can compile and run the application to display video content within a Swing window. By executing the Java command with the appropriate classpath and specifying the VideoPlayer class as the main class, developers can launch the Swing application and view the video content within the application window.

bashCopy code

```
java -classpath jmf.jar:. VideoPlayer
```

In this command, "jmf.jar" represents the JMF library file, and "VideoPlayer" is the name of the Java class containing the code for displaying video content. By including the JMF library in the classpath and specifying the VideoPlayer class as the main class, developers can launch the Swing application and display video content within the application window.

Furthermore, developers can customize the video playback experience by adjusting various parameters of the Player object, such as volume, playback speed, and visual rendering options. Additionally, JMF supports advanced features such as streaming media, video capture, and multimedia synchronization, allowing developers to create sophisticated multimedia applications with ease.

In summary, displaying video content with JMF in Swing applications is a powerful technique for creating interactive and immersive multimedia experiences. By leveraging JMF's comprehensive API and libraries, developers can integrate video playback functionality seamlessly into Java applications, providing users with compelling visual content and enhancing the overall user experience. With its support for various multimedia formats and advanced features, JMF enables developers to create sophisticated multimedia applications that captivate and engage users effectively.

## Chapter 9: Internationalization and Localization

Supporting multiple languages in software applications is crucial for reaching a diverse user base and ensuring inclusivity. ResourceBundle, a part of the Java Internationalization (i18n) framework, offers a convenient mechanism for managing localized resources such as strings, images, and other data in different languages. By utilizing ResourceBundle effectively, developers can create applications that adapt seamlessly to users' language preferences, providing a more personalized and user-friendly experience.

To begin leveraging ResourceBundle for multilingual support in a Java application, developers typically create resource bundles containing translations for various languages. A resource bundle is a set of key-value pairs where each key corresponds to a specific resource, such as a string or image, and its value represents the translation or localized version of that resource in a particular language.

The process starts by creating separate properties files for each supported language, following a standardized naming convention that includes the base name of the resource bundle and the language code. For example, a resource bundle named "Messages" would have properties files named "Messages.properties" for the default language (usually English) and "Messages_fr.properties" for French translations.

bashCopy code

```
# Create properties files for English and French translations touch Messages.properties Messages_fr.properties
```

In this command, "touch" is a command-line utility used to create empty files. Developers should replace "fr" with the appropriate language code for other supported languages.

Once the properties files are created, developers can populate them with key-value pairs representing the localized resources for each language. For instance, in the "Messages.properties" file, developers would define key-value pairs for English translations, while the "Messages_fr.properties" file would contain French translations.

makefileCopy code

```
# Messages.properties (English translations) greeting=Hello farewell=Goodbye # Messages_fr.properties (French translations) greeting=Bonjour farewell=Au revoir
```

In these files, "greeting" and "farewell" are keys representing localized messages in English and French, respectively. Developers should provide translations for all supported languages in their respective properties files.

Once the resource bundles are defined, developers can load them into their Java application using the ResourceBundle class. ResourceBundle provides methods for accessing localized resources based on the user's locale, automatically selecting the appropriate resource bundle based on the user's language preference.

javaCopy code

```
// Load the default resource bundle (Messages.properties) ResourceBundle bundle = ResourceBundle.getBundle("Messages"); // Load the resource bundle for a specific locale (e.g., French) ResourceBundle frenchBundle = ResourceBundle.getBundle("Messages", new Locale("fr"));
```

In this Java code snippet, developers use the ResourceBundle.getBundle() method to load the resource bundle for the default locale (usually the system default) and a specific locale (e.g., French). ResourceBundle automatically selects the appropriate properties file based on the locale specified, allowing developers to retrieve localized resources dynamically.

Once the resource bundle is loaded, developers can retrieve localized resources using their corresponding keys.

javaCopy code

```
// Retrieve localized messages String greeting = bundle.getString("greeting"); String farewell = bundle.getString("farewell");
```

In this code snippet, the getString() method is used to retrieve the localized messages for the "greeting" and "farewell" keys from the resource bundle. ResourceBundle handles the retrieval of the appropriate translation based on the selected locale, ensuring that users receive content in their preferred language.

By leveraging ResourceBundle for multilingual support, developers can create applications that cater to users from diverse linguistic backgrounds, enhancing accessibility and usability. ResourceBundle simplifies the process of managing localized resources and provides a flexible solution for adapting applications to different languages without requiring significant code changes.

Furthermore, ResourceBundle supports fallback mechanisms, allowing developers to specify default values for keys in case translations are missing for a particular language. This ensures a smooth user experience even when translations are incomplete or unavailable for certain languages.

Overall, ResourceBundle is a powerful tool for supporting multiple languages in Java applications, enabling developers to create inclusive and user-friendly software experiences that resonate with global audiences. By following best practices for resource bundle management and localization, developers can leverage ResourceBundle to deliver personalized and engaging experiences tailored to users' language preferences.

Formatting dates, numbers, and currencies for different locales is a fundamental aspect of internationalization (i18n) in software development, essential for creating applications that cater to diverse cultural and linguistic preferences. In Java, the java.text package provides classes such as DateFormat, NumberFormat, and CurrencyFormat, which enable developers to format and parse dates, numbers, and currencies according to specific locale conventions. By leveraging these classes effectively, developers can ensure that their applications present information consistently and accurately across different regions and languages.

To begin formatting dates, numbers, and currencies for different locales in a Java application, developers typically create instances of the DateFormat, NumberFormat, and CurrencyFormat classes, specifying the desired locale for formatting and parsing operations. These classes provide various methods for formatting and parsing data according to locale-specific conventions, allowing developers to customize the presentation of dates, numbers, and currencies based on regional preferences.

For example, to format dates according to the conventions of a specific locale, developers can create an instance of the DateFormat class and set its locale property to the desired locale.

javaCopy code

```
// Create a DateFormat instance for the default locale DateFormat dateFormat = DateFormat.getDateInstance(DateFormat.FULL); // Create a DateFormat instance for a specific locale (e.g., French) DateFormat frenchDateFormat = DateFormat.getDateInstance(DateFormat.FULL, Locale.FRENCH);
```

In this Java code snippet, the getDateInstance() method of the DateFormat class is used to create DateFormat instances for the default locale and a specific locale (e.g., French). By passing the DateFormat.FULL constant, developers specify that the DateFormat instance should format dates using the full date style appropriate for the specified locale.

Once the DateFormat instances are created, developers can format dates using their format() method, passing a Date object representing the date to be formatted.

javaCopy code

```
// Format a date using the default locale String formattedDate = dateFormat.format(new Date()); // Format a date using the French locale String frenchFormattedDate = frenchDateFormat.format(new Date());
```

In these code snippets, the format() method of the DateFormat instances is used to format a Date object representing the current date according to the conventions of the default locale and the French locale, respectively. The formatted dates are returned as strings suitable for display to users.

Similarly, to format numbers and currencies for different locales, developers can create instances of the NumberFormat and CurrencyFormat classes, specifying the desired locale for formatting operations.

javaCopy code

```
// Create a NumberFormat instance for the default locale NumberFormat numberFormat = NumberFormat.getNumberInstance(); // Create a NumberFormat instance for a specific locale (e.g., German) NumberFormat germanNumberFormat = NumberFormat.getNumberInstance(Locale.GERMAN);
// Create a CurrencyFormat instance for the default locale CurrencyFormat currencyFormat =
```

CurrencyFormat.getCurrencyInstance(); // Create a CurrencyFormat instance for a specific locale (e.g., Japanese) CurrencyFormat japaneseCurrencyFormat = CurrencyFormat.getCurrencyInstance(Locale.JAPANESE );

In these Java code snippets, instances of the NumberFormat and CurrencyFormat classes are created for the default locale and specific locales (e.g., German and Japanese). By specifying the desired locale, developers ensure that number and currency formatting operations adhere to the conventions of the selected locale. Once the NumberFormat and CurrencyFormat instances are created, developers can format numbers and currencies using their format() method, passing numeric or currency values to be formatted.

javaCopy code

// Format a number using the default locale String formattedNumber = numberFormat.format( 12345.67 ); // Format a number using the German locale String germanFormattedNumber = germanNumberFormat.format( 12345.67 ); // Format a currency using the default locale String formattedCurrency = currencyFormat.format( 12345.67 ); // Format a currency using the Japanese locale String japaneseFormattedCurrency = japaneseCurrencyFormat.format( 12345.67 );

In these code snippets, the format() method of the NumberFormat and CurrencyFormat instances is used to format numeric and currency values according to the conventions of the default locale and specific locales. The formatted numbers and currencies are returned as strings suitable for display to users.

By utilizing DateFormat, NumberFormat, and CurrencyFormat classes in conjunction with locale-specific settings, developers can ensure that their applications present dates, numbers, and currencies consistently and accurately across different regions and languages. This approach facilitates the creation of internationalized applications that cater to the diverse needs and preferences of users worldwide, enhancing usability and accessibility.

Furthermore, Java provides mechanisms for customizing date, number, and currency formatting patterns to accommodate specific requirements or preferences. Developers can use methods such as setDateFormatSymbols() and setDecimalFormatSymbols() to customize formatting symbols such as month names, currency symbols, and decimal separators according to locale-specific conventions.

javaCopy code

```
// Customize date format symbols for the default locale
DateFormatSymbols dateFormatSymbols = new
DateFormatSymbols();
dateFormatSymbols.setMonths(new String[]{"Jan",
"Feb", "Mar", "Apr", "May", "Jun", "Jul", "Aug",
```

"Sep", "Oct", "Nov", "Dec"}); dateFormat.setDateFormatSymbols(dateFormatSymbols); // Customize number format symbols for the default locale DecimalFormatSymbols decimalFormatSymbols = new DecimalFormatSymbols(); decimalFormatSymbols.setDecimalSeparator(','); decimalFormat.setDecimalFormatSymbols(decimalFormatSymbols); // Customize currency format symbols for the default locale Currency currency = Currency.getInstance(Locale.US); currencyFormat.setCurrency(currency);

In this Java code snippet, the setDateFormatSymbols(), setDecimalFormatSymbols(), and setCurrency() methods are used to customize date, number, and currency formatting symbols for the default locale. Developers can specify custom symbols such as month names, decimal separators, and currency symbols to tailor formatting output to specific requirements or preferences. Overall, formatting dates, numbers, and currencies for different locales is essential for creating internationalized applications that cater to diverse linguistic and cultural preferences. By leveraging DateFormat, NumberFormat, and CurrencyFormat classes in conjunction with locale-specific settings, developers can ensure that their applications provide consistent and accurate representations of dates, numbers, and currencies across different regions and languages, enhancing usability, accessibility, and user satisfaction.

## Chapter 10: Accessibility Features in Swing Applications

Implementing screen reader support with AccessibleContext is a critical aspect of creating accessible applications for users with visual impairments or disabilities. AccessibleContext, a class in the Java Accessibility API, provides a standardized way for developers to expose information about user interface components to assistive technologies like screen readers. By leveraging AccessibleContext effectively, developers can ensure that their applications are navigable and usable by individuals who rely on screen readers to interact with graphical user interfaces.

To implement screen reader support with AccessibleContext in a Java application, developers typically extend existing user interface components such as buttons, labels, and text fields to provide additional accessibility information. These components must override methods defined by the AccessibleContext class to expose relevant properties, actions, and state information to assistive technologies.

For example, to create a custom accessible button component, developers can extend the JButton class and override methods from the AccessibleContext class to provide accessibility information.

javaCopy code

import javax.accessibility.Accessible; import javax.accessibility.AccessibleContext; import javax.swing.JButton; public class AccessibleButton extends JButton implements Accessible { public AccessibleButton(String text) { super(text); } @Override public AccessibleContext getAccessibleContext() { if (accessibleContext == null) { accessibleContext = new AccessibleButtonContext(); } return accessibleContext; } protected class AccessibleButtonContext extends AccessibleJButton { @Override public String getAccessibleName() { // Provide a descriptive name for the button return "Custom Accessible Button"; } @Override public String getAccessibleDescription() { // Provide additional description for the button return "This is a custom button with accessibility support."; } // Override other AccessibleContext methods as needed } }

In this Java code snippet, a custom AccessibleButton class is defined by extending the JButton class and implementing the Accessible interface. The getAccessibleContext() method is overridden to return an instance of a custom AccessibleButtonContext class, which extends AccessibleJButton, a default implementation of the AccessibleContext interface provided by Swing.

Within the AccessibleButtonContext class, developers can override methods such as getAccessibleName() and getAccessibleDescription() to provide descriptive information about the custom button component.

These methods allow developers to specify the name, description, and other accessibility attributes that assistive technologies can use to convey information to users with disabilities.

Once the custom accessible components are implemented, developers can incorporate them into their application's user interface, ensuring that users with visual impairments can interact with the application effectively using screen readers.

javaCopy code

```
public class MainApplication { public static void main(String[] args) { // Create a frame and add the custom accessible button JFrame frame = new JFrame("Accessible Application"); AccessibleButton button = new AccessibleButton("Click Me"); frame.add(button); frame.pack(); frame.setVisible(true); } }
```

In this Java code snippet, a MainApplication class is defined to create a Swing frame and add the custom accessible button component to it. By adding accessible components to the user interface and providing appropriate accessibility information through the AccessibleContext interface, developers can ensure that their applications are accessible to users with visual impairments or disabilities.

Additionally, developers should test their accessible components with screen reader software to verify that the information exposed through AccessibleContext is conveyed accurately and effectively to users. This iterative testing process helps identify and address

accessibility issues, ensuring that the application provides a seamless and inclusive user experience for all users.
Overall, implementing screen reader support with AccessibleContext is essential for creating accessible applications that accommodate users with visual impairments or disabilities. By extending user interface components to provide accessibility information through the AccessibleContext interface, developers can enhance the usability and inclusivity of their applications, ensuring that all users can interact with them effectively using screen readers and other assistive technologies.

Enabling keyboard navigation for accessibility is a crucial aspect of creating inclusive software applications that cater to users with mobility impairments or those who prefer keyboard input over mouse interaction. Keyboard navigation allows users to navigate through the application interface, interact with elements, and perform actions solely using keyboard inputs, enhancing accessibility and usability. In Java applications, implementing keyboard navigation involves ensuring that all interactive elements are accessible via keyboard shortcuts or tab navigation, providing users with alternative methods to navigate and interact with the application.
One fundamental aspect of enabling keyboard navigation is defining keyboard shortcuts for frequently used actions within the application. These shortcuts allow users to perform tasks without relying on mouse

interactions, improving efficiency and accessibility. In Java Swing applications, developers can define keyboard shortcuts using the setMnemonic() or setAccelerator() methods available in components such as buttons, menu items, and other interactive elements. For example, to create a button with a keyboard shortcut in a Java Swing application, developers can use the setMnemonic() method to assign a mnemonic key to the button.

javaCopy code

```
JButton button = new JButton("Submit");
button.setMnemonic(KeyEvent.VK_S); // Assigns Alt + S as the mnemonic key
```

In this code snippet, the setMnemonic() method is used to assign the Alt + S combination as the mnemonic key for the button, allowing users to trigger the button action by pressing Alt + S on the keyboard. Similarly, developers can define keyboard shortcuts for menu items, text fields, and other components using the setAccelerator() method, which allows users to activate actions using key combinations such as Ctrl + key or Ctrl + Shift + key.

Another essential aspect of enabling keyboard navigation is implementing focus traversal. Focus traversal ensures that users can navigate between interactive elements in the application using the keyboard's Tab and Shift + Tab keys. In Java Swing applications, focus traversal is facilitated by the FocusTraversalPolicy class, which defines the order in which components receive focus when the user navigates using the Tab key.

javaCopy code

```
// Define custom focus traversal policy
FocusTraversalPolicy policy = new
CustomFocusTraversalPolicy(); // Set the focus
traversal policy for the container
container.setFocusTraversalPolicy(policy);
```

In this code snippet, a CustomFocusTraversalPolicy class is created to define the custom focus traversal order for components within a container. By setting the custom focus traversal policy using the setFocusTraversalPolicy() method, developers can control the tab order and ensure that keyboard navigation follows a logical sequence that aligns with the application's user interface.

Additionally, developers should ensure that all interactive elements within the application are accessible via keyboard navigation, allowing users to interact with buttons, checkboxes, radio buttons, and other controls using the keyboard alone. This includes providing keyboard shortcuts for accessing menu items, navigating between form fields, and activating context menus or dialogs.

Furthermore, developers should consider providing visual indicators, such as focus rectangles or highlight colors, to indicate the currently focused element when navigating using the keyboard. These visual cues help users maintain context and understand which element is currently selected for interaction.

Testing keyboard navigation is crucial to ensure that the application is accessible and usable for users who rely on keyboard input. Developers should conduct thorough testing with keyboard-only interactions, verifying that all interactive elements are accessible and that focus traversal follows an intuitive sequence. This testing process helps identify and address any accessibility issues or usability challenges related to keyboard navigation, ensuring that the application provides a seamless and inclusive experience for all users.

Overall, enabling keyboard navigation for accessibility in Java applications is essential for creating inclusive software that accommodates users with mobility impairments or those who prefer keyboard input. By defining keyboard shortcuts, implementing focus traversal, and ensuring accessibility of interactive elements, developers can enhance the usability and accessibility of their applications, providing an inclusive user experience for all users.

***BOOK 3***

***ADVANCED JAVA SWING DEVELOPMENT***

***BUILDING DYNAMIC AND RESPONSIVE GUIS***

***ROB BOTWRIGHT***

## Chapter 1: Introduction to Advanced Swing Development

Exploring advanced Swing features delves into the rich capabilities of the Swing framework, offering developers a deeper understanding of its functionalities and empowering them to create more sophisticated and feature-rich graphical user interfaces (GUIs). These advanced features extend beyond the basics of Swing programming, providing developers with tools and techniques to tackle complex UI design challenges and implement innovative solutions in their Java applications. By leveraging these advanced features, developers can enhance the visual appeal, interactivity, and usability of their Swing-based applications, delivering compelling user experiences that meet the demands of modern software development.

One advanced Swing feature worth exploring is the JLayeredPane component, which allows developers to create layered user interfaces with overlapping components. JLayeredPane provides a flexible and powerful mechanism for managing the z-order of components within a container, enabling developers to overlay components, such as images, panels, or custom widgets, to create visually dynamic and interactive UIs. To utilize JLayeredPane, developers can instantiate an instance of the JLayeredPane class and add components to specific layers using the setLayer() method.

javaCopy code

```
JLayeredPane layeredPane = new JLayeredPane(); layeredPane.add(component1,
JLayeredPane.DEFAULT_LAYER); // Adds component1 to the default layer layeredPane.add(component2, JLayeredPane.PALETTE_LAYER); // Adds component2 to the palette layer
```

In this example, component1 and component2 are added to the JLayeredPane with different layer values, allowing developers to control the stacking order of components within the container. By leveraging JLayeredPane, developers can create visually compelling interfaces with complex layouts and layered elements, enhancing the overall user experience of their Swing applications.

Another advanced Swing feature is the SwingWorker API, which facilitates concurrent programming and asynchronous task execution within Swing applications. SwingWorker allows developers to perform time-consuming tasks, such as data processing or network operations, in the background without freezing the UI thread, ensuring that the application remains responsive and maintains a smooth user experience. To use SwingWorker, developers can subclass the SwingWorker class and override the doInBackground() method to define the background task, as well as the done() method to handle the task completion.

javaCopy code

```
SwingWorker<Integer, Void> worker = new SwingWorker<Integer, Void>() { @Override protected Integer doInBackground() throws Exception { //
```

Perform time-consuming task in the background return performTimeConsumingTask(); } @Override protected void done() { try { // Handle task completion int result = get(); // Update UI with result } catch (InterruptedException | ExecutionException ex) { ex.printStackTrace(); } } }; worker.execute(); // Executes the SwingWorker

By utilizing the SwingWorker API, developers can improve the responsiveness and performance of their Swing applications, enabling them to handle complex computations or I/O operations without impacting the user interface's fluidity and responsiveness.

Additionally, developers can explore advanced layout management techniques, such as GroupLayout and GridBagLayout, to create flexible and responsive UI layouts that adapt to different screen sizes and resolutions. GroupLayout offers a versatile and intuitive way to design complex layouts with nested groups and alignment constraints, while GridBagLayout provides fine-grained control over component positioning and sizing within a grid-based layout structure.

javaCopy code

```
GroupLayout layout = new GroupLayout(container);
container.setLayout(layout);
layout.setAutoCreateGaps(true);
layout.setAutoCreateContainerGaps(true); // Define horizontal and vertical groups layout.setHorizontalGroup(layout.createSequentialGroup() .addComponent(component1)
```

```
.addComponent(component2)
.addGroup(layout.createParallelGroup(GroupLayout.Ali
gnment.LEADING)         .addComponent(component3)
.addComponent(component4))                          );
layout.setVerticalGroup(layout.createSequentialGroup(
)
.addGroup(layout.createParallelGroup(GroupLayout.Ali
gnment.BASELINE)        .addComponent(component1)
.addComponent(component2))
.addGroup(layout.createParallelGroup(GroupLayout.Ali
gnment.LEADING)        .addComponent(component3))
.addComponent(component4) );
```

In this example, a GroupLayout is used to define the horizontal and vertical groups for a container, specifying the arrangement and alignment of components within the layout. By leveraging advanced layout management techniques like GroupLayout and GridBagLayout, developers can create UIs with precise control over component placement and alignment, ensuring a polished and professional appearance across different platforms and devices.

Furthermore, developers can explore advanced painting and rendering techniques, such as custom painting with the Java 2D API or integrating 3D graphics with Java 3D, to create visually stunning and immersive user interfaces. Custom painting allows developers to create custom graphics and visual effects directly on Swing components, while Java 3D enables the integration of three-dimensional models and animations into Swing applications, opening up new possibilities for interactive and engaging user experiences.

javaCopy code

```java
@Override protected void paintComponent(Graphics g) { super.paintComponent(g); Graphics2D g2d = (Graphics2D) g.create(); // Perform custom painting operations g2d.setColor(Color.RED); g2d.fillRect(0, 0, getWidth(), getHeight()); g2d.dispose(); }
```

In this example, the paintComponent() method is overridden to perform custom painting operations, such as drawing shapes or rendering images, directly on the component's surface using the Graphics2D API. By harnessing the power of custom painting and 3D graphics, developers can create visually stunning and immersive user interfaces that captivate and engage users, elevating the overall user experience of their Swing applications.

Moreover, developers can explore advanced event handling techniques, such as implementing drag-and-drop functionality or supporting multi-touch gestures, to enhance the interactivity and usability of their Swing applications. Drag-and-drop allows users to intuitively manipulate and rearrange components within the UI by dragging them with the mouse or touch input, while multi-touch gestures enable users to interact with the application using multiple fingers or touch points simultaneously.

javaCopy code

```java
// Enable drag-and-drop functionality component.setTransferHandler(new
```

TransferHandler("text")); // Implement drag-and-drop gesture recognition component.addMouseMotionListener(new MouseAdapter() { public void mouseDragged(MouseEvent e) { TransferHandler handler = component.getTransferHandler(); if (handler != null) { handler.exportAsDrag(component, e, TransferHandler.COPY); } } });

In this example, drag-and-drop functionality is enabled for a Swing component by setting a TransferHandler, which defines the data transfer mechanism for drag-and-drop operations. By implementing mouse motion listeners and drag gesture recognition, developers can create intuitive drag-and-drop interactions that empower users to manipulate and organize UI elements effortlessly.

Additionally, developers can leverage multi-touch gesture recognition libraries, such as MT4J or JavaFX, to support advanced touch-based interactions in Swing applications. These libraries provide APIs for detecting and handling multi-touch gestures, such as pinch-to-zoom or swipe-to-scroll, enabling developers to create touch-friendly interfaces that deliver a seamless and immersive user experience on touch-enabled devices.

In summary, exploring advanced Swing features equips developers with the tools and techniques needed to create sophisticated and visually appealing user interfaces in Java applications. By leveraging features such as JLayeredPane for layered UI design, SwingWorker for concurrent programming, advanced layout managers for responsive UI layouts, custom painting for visual effects, and advanced event handling for intuitive interactions, developers can elevate the usability, interactivity, and accessibility of their Swing-based applications, delivering compelling user experiences that meet the expectations of modern software users.

Understanding the evolution of Swing architecture provides valuable insights into the development and maturation of Java's graphical user interface (GUI) toolkit, offering developers a deeper understanding of its underlying design principles, components, and capabilities. Swing, introduced as part of the Java Foundation Classes (JFC) in the late 1990s, revolutionized GUI development in Java by providing a platform-independent framework for building rich and interactive user interfaces across various operating systems and devices. Over the years, Swing has undergone significant evolution and refinement, driven by advancements in technology, changes in user expectations, and feedback from the developer community.

The roots of Swing can be traced back to the Abstract Window Toolkit (AWT), Java's original GUI toolkit, which provided basic support for creating GUI components and handling user events. However, AWT had limitations, particularly in terms of its look and feel, as it relied heavily on native platform components, resulting in inconsistent user experiences across different operating systems. Recognizing the need for a more flexible and customizable GUI framework, Sun Microsystems (now Oracle Corporation) introduced Swing as part of the Java Foundation Classes (JFC) in JDK 1.2.

Swing was designed from the ground up to address the shortcomings of AWT while providing developers with a comprehensive set of GUI components, layout managers, and event handling mechanisms. Unlike AWT, Swing components are lightweight, meaning they are implemented entirely in Java and do not rely on native platform resources for rendering. This architectural decision enabled Swing to achieve platform independence and consistent behavior across different operating systems, a key advantage over its predecessor.

One of the defining features of Swing architecture is its Model-View-Controller (MVC) design pattern, which separates the presentation (view) of GUI components from their data (model) and event handling (controller) logic. This separation of concerns allows developers to create modular and reusable GUI components, promoting code maintainability and flexibility. Swing components typically follow this MVC pattern, with each component having a corresponding model class that manages its data and a controller class that handles user interactions and events.

Moreover, Swing introduced a pluggable look and feel (PLAF) mechanism, which allows developers to customize the appearance and behavior of GUI components by choosing from a variety of available look and feel implementations or creating their own. This flexibility enables developers to create UIs that match the native look and feel of the underlying platform or design custom themes to suit their application's branding and aesthetic preferences.

As Swing continued to evolve, subsequent updates and releases introduced new features, enhancements, and performance improvements to meet the evolving needs of developers and users. For example, the introduction of the SwingWorker API in JDK 6 provided a standardized way to perform background tasks and asynchronous operations within Swing applications, addressing common concurrency challenges and improving the responsiveness of GUIs.

Furthermore, Swing has embraced modern design paradigms and integration with other Java technologies, such as JavaFX, to offer developers more options for creating modern and visually appealing user interfaces.

While Swing remains a robust and widely used GUI toolkit in Java development, newer technologies like JavaFX have emerged, offering advanced features, hardware acceleration, and a more declarative approach to UI design.

Despite the emergence of new technologies, Swing continues to be actively maintained and supported by the Java community, with ongoing efforts to improve performance, compatibility, and developer productivity.

The enduring popularity of Swing can be attributed to its stability, maturity, and extensive ecosystem of third-party libraries, tools, and resources that support Swing development.

In summary, understanding the evolution of Swing architecture provides developers with valuable insights into the design principles, features, and capabilities of Java's primary GUI toolkit. From its origins as an improvement over AWT to its continued relevance in modern Java development, Swing has played a significant role in shaping the landscape of GUI programming in Java. By understanding Swing's architecture and evolution, developers can leverage its strengths to create robust, platform-independent GUI applications that deliver compelling user experiences.

## Chapter 2: Implementing Advanced Event Handling

Understanding event propagation in Swing components is essential for developing responsive and interactive user interfaces in Java applications. When a user interacts with a Swing component, such as clicking a button or typing in a text field, the corresponding events need to be propagated through the component hierarchy to ensure that the appropriate listeners are notified and can respond accordingly. This process of event propagation follows a hierarchical pattern, starting from the component where the event originated and propagating upwards through its parent and ancestor components until reaching the root of the component hierarchy.

At the core of event propagation in Swing is the Event Dispatch Thread (EDT), a dedicated thread responsible for processing and dispatching events within a Swing application. All GUI-related events, including user input events and component-specific events, are processed on the EDT to ensure thread safety and prevent potential concurrency issues. When an event occurs, such as a button click or mouse movement, it is initially captured by the native platform's event system and forwarded to the corresponding Swing component for processing.

Once the event reaches the Swing component, it undergoes a process known as event dispatching, where it is dispatched to the appropriate event listeners registered on the component. Event listeners are interfaces or classes that implement specific event-handling methods, such as actionPerformed() for action events or keyPressed() for key events, allowing developers to define custom behavior for handling different types of events. By registering event listeners on Swing components, developers can specify how the application should respond to user interactions and input events.

During event dispatching, Swing components follow a predefined order known as the event propagation hierarchy, which determines the sequence in which events are delivered to listeners. The event propagation hierarchy is based on the containment hierarchy of Swing components, where events are first delivered to the target component where the event occurred and then propagated upwards through its parent and ancestor components. This hierarchical propagation ensures that events are delivered to the appropriate listeners in the component hierarchy, allowing for fine-grained control over event handling and propagation.

In addition to the target component, events may also be intercepted and processed by intermediate components along the event propagation path, such as event listeners registered on parent or ancestor components. This allows developers to implement event-handling logic at different levels of the component hierarchy, enabling them to respond to events globally or within specific regions of the UI. For example, a mouse click event on a button may trigger action listeners registered on both the button itself and its parent panel, allowing developers to perform additional processing or validation logic at the panel level.

Furthermore, Swing provides mechanisms for controlling event propagation and preventing event bubbling or propagation to higher-level components. For example, the consume() method can be called on certain types of events to indicate that the event has been fully processed and should not be propagated further. Similarly, event listeners can consume events by returning true from their event-handling methods, indicating that the event has been consumed and should not be processed by other listeners.

Understanding event propagation in Swing components is crucial for developing robust and responsive GUI applications in Java. By mastering the principles of event dispatching and propagation, developers can create dynamic and interactive user interfaces that respond seamlessly to user input and interactions. Whether handling simple button clicks or complex mouse movements, event propagation in Swing provides a solid foundation for building intuitive and engaging user experiences in Java applications. Implementing custom event classes and listeners is a fundamental aspect of event-driven programming in Java Swing, allowing developers to create custom event types and define how components interact and communicate within a GUI application. While Swing provides a rich set of built-in events and listeners for common user interactions, such as button clicks and mouse movements, there are scenarios where developers need to define custom events to handle application-specific interactions or data updates. By creating custom event classes and listeners, developers can extend the capabilities of Swing components and enable more flexible and tailored event handling mechanisms.

To implement custom event classes and listeners in Swing, developers typically follow a few key steps. First, they define the custom event class by creating a subclass of the java.util.EventObject class, which serves as the base class for all event objects in Java. The custom event class encapsulates relevant data or state changes associated with the event and provides methods for accessing this information. For example, a custom event class for handling temperature updates in a weather application might include methods for retrieving the updated temperature value and the location where the update occurred.

Once the custom event class is defined, developers need to create corresponding listener interfaces or classes that define how components respond to the custom events. Listener interfaces typically extend java.util.EventListener and declare methods for handling specific types of events. For example, a TemperatureChangeListener interface might define a method like temperatureChanged(TemperatureChangeEvent event) to handle temperature update events. Alternatively, developers can create listener classes that implement the listener interfaces and provide concrete implementations for event-handling methods.

After defining the custom event class and listener interfaces or classes, developers can integrate them into their Swing application by registering event listeners on the appropriate components and dispatching custom events when necessary. This typically involves adding methods to components for registering and unregistering event listeners and dispatching custom events using the javax.swing.event.EventListenerList and java.awt.EventQueue classes. For example, a TemperatureSensor component might expose methods like addTemperatureChangeListener() and fireTemperatureChangeEvent() to allow other components to register listeners and receive temperature update events.

When dispatching custom events, developers should ensure that events are dispatched on the Event Dispatch Thread (EDT) to maintain thread safety and prevent potential concurrency issues. This can be achieved by wrapping event dispatching code in javax.swing.SwingUtilities.invokeLater() or javax.swing.SwingUtilities.invokeAndWait() methods, which schedule tasks to be executed asynchronously or synchronously on the EDT, respectively. By dispatching events on the EDT, developers can ensure that event-handling code executes in a consistent and predictable manner, regardless of the underlying platform or threading model.

In addition to dispatching custom events, developers should also implement event-handling logic in event listener methods to respond to events appropriately. This may involve updating the state of components, triggering UI updates, or performing additional processing based on the event data. For example, a TemperatureChangeListener might update the display of temperature information in a GUI panel in response to temperature update events received from a TemperatureSensor component.

Furthermore, developers should consider best practices for naming conventions, documentation, and error handling when implementing custom event classes and listeners. Meaningful and descriptive class and method names can improve code readability and maintainability, while clear documentation helps other developers understand how to use the custom events and listeners in their own code. Additionally, proper error handling ensures that applications gracefully handle unexpected conditions and provide informative error messages to users when necessary.

In summary, implementing custom event classes and listeners in Java Swing is a powerful technique for extending the event-driven architecture of Swing applications and enabling more flexible and tailored event handling mechanisms. By defining custom event classes, creating listener interfaces or classes, and integrating them into Swing components, developers can enhance the responsiveness and interactivity of GUI applications and provide a richer user experience. Whether handling application-specific interactions or responding to data updates, custom events and listeners play a crucial role in the development of sophisticated and dynamic Swing applications.

## Chapter 3: Dynamic GUI Updates with SwingWorkers

Background processing with SwingWorker is a fundamental aspect of developing responsive and efficient Swing applications in Java. Swing applications often need to perform time-consuming tasks, such as network communication, file I/O, or database queries, without blocking the Event Dispatch Thread (EDT) to maintain a smooth and responsive user interface. SwingWorker provides a convenient and thread-safe way to execute such tasks in the background while keeping the EDT free to handle user interactions and update the GUI.

To utilize SwingWorker in a Java application, developers typically create a subclass of SwingWorker<T, V>, where T represents the result type of the background task and V represents the type used for intermediate results or progress updates. The doInBackground() method, overridden in the subclass, contains the code that executes the time-consuming task in a separate background thread. This method runs outside the EDT, ensuring that it does not block the UI and allows the application to remain responsive.

Meanwhile, developers can optionally override other methods, such as process() and done(), to handle intermediate results and post-processing tasks, respectively. The process() method receives intermediate results generated by the background task and updates the GUI accordingly, typically by publishing them to components or data structures that are accessible from the EDT. This allows developers to provide real-time feedback or progress updates to users while the background task is executing.

The done() method, on the other hand, is invoked once the background task completes, either successfully or due to cancellation or error. This method runs on the EDT and provides an opportunity for developers to perform any post-processing tasks, such as updating the UI with the final result or handling exceptions that may have occurred during the background task execution.

To execute a SwingWorker instance, developers typically create an instance of the subclass and invoke its execute() method. This method initiates the background task by spawning a separate thread to execute the doInBackground() method, ensuring that the EDT remains unblocked and responsive to user interactions.

One of the key advantages of using SwingWorker is its support for concurrency and thread safety. By handling background tasks in separate threads, SwingWorker helps prevent blocking the EDT, ensuring that the application remains responsive even when performing lengthy operations. Moreover, SwingWorker provides built-in mechanisms for safely updating the GUI from background threads, such as the publish() and process() methods, which help prevent potential concurrency issues and synchronization problems.

Another important feature of SwingWorker is its support for cancellation and progress monitoring. Developers can use the cancel() method to interrupt the background task if needed, allowing users to cancel long-running operations or providing a means to gracefully abort tasks that are no longer needed. Additionally, SwingWorker provides methods for tracking the progress of background tasks, such as setProgress() and getProgress(), allowing developers to provide visual feedback or progress indicators to users during task execution.

Overall, SwingWorker is an essential tool for implementing background processing in Swing applications, enabling developers to create responsive and efficient user interfaces that can handle time-consuming tasks without sacrificing usability or performance. By leveraging SwingWorker, developers can ensure that their applications remain responsive and maintain a smooth user experience even when performing complex operations in the background.

Updating Swing components asynchronously is a crucial aspect of developing responsive and dynamic user interfaces in Java applications. Swing, being a single-threaded framework, requires careful handling of GUI updates to prevent blocking the Event Dispatch Thread (EDT), which is responsible for processing user input and updating the UI. Asynchronous updates allow developers to perform time-consuming operations in the background while keeping the UI responsive and maintaining a smooth user experience.

One common scenario where asynchronous updating of Swing components is necessary is when fetching data from external sources, such as databases, web services, or files. These operations can introduce delays, potentially causing the UI to become unresponsive if performed on the EDT. To address this issue, developers can use various techniques to update Swing components asynchronously, ensuring that the UI remains interactive even during lengthy data retrieval or processing tasks.

One approach to asynchronous updating is to use SwingWorker, as discussed earlier. By subclassing SwingWorker and overriding its doInBackground() method to perform the data retrieval or processing task in a background thread, developers can keep the EDT free to handle user interactions. Once the background task completes, the SwingWorker's done() method, running on the EDT, can update the UI with the retrieved or processed data, ensuring a responsive and smooth user experience.

Another technique for asynchronous updating is to use the javax.swing.Timer class, which allows developers to schedule periodic or one-time tasks to be executed on the EDT after a specified delay. By using a Timer, developers can periodically check for updates from external sources and update the UI accordingly without blocking the EDT. For example, a Timer can be used to fetch real-time data from a web service and update a Swing component with the latest information at regular intervals.

In addition to SwingWorker and Timer, developers can also use Java's concurrency utilities, such as java.util.concurrent.ExecutorService and java.util.concurrent.Future, to perform asynchronous tasks and update Swing components. These utilities provide more flexibility and control over thread management and task execution, allowing developers to fine-tune the concurrency behavior of their applications to suit specific requirements.

When updating Swing components asynchronously, developers must ensure proper synchronization and coordination between the background threads and the EDT to prevent concurrency issues and race conditions. Swing provides mechanisms for safely updating the UI from background threads, such as the javax.swing.SwingUtilities.invokeLater() and javax.swing.SwingUtilities.invokeAndWait() methods, which allow developers to enqueue UI updates on the EDT's event queue for later execution.

Furthermore, developers should consider implementing techniques such as data caching, result caching, and lazy loading to optimize the performance of asynchronous updates and minimize unnecessary data retrieval or processing. By caching previously fetched data or computed results, developers can reduce the frequency of updates and improve the responsiveness of the UI, especially in scenarios where data access or computation is resource-intensive.

Overall, updating Swing components asynchronously is essential for creating responsive and dynamic user interfaces in Java applications. By leveraging techniques such as SwingWorker, Timer, and concurrency utilities, developers can perform time-consuming operations in the background while keeping the UI responsive and maintaining a smooth user experience. With proper synchronization and optimization, asynchronous updating enables developers to build robust and efficient Swing applications that meet the demands of modern user interface design.

## Chapter 4: Advanced Layout Techniques for Responsive UIs

Flexbox layout in Java Swing is a modern approach to designing flexible and responsive user interfaces, inspired by the CSS Flexible Box Layout Module. This layout model provides developers with powerful tools for creating complex layouts that adapt dynamically to different screen sizes and orientations, offering greater flexibility and consistency across various devices and platforms. While Swing traditionally relies on layout managers like BorderLayout, GridLayout, and BoxLayout, which offer limited flexibility and control over component positioning and resizing, Flexbox layout introduces a more intuitive and powerful paradigm for building sophisticated UIs.

To implement Flexbox layout in Java Swing, developers can leverage third-party libraries such as MigLayout or FlexLayout, which provide robust support for Flexbox-style layout management. These libraries offer a comprehensive set of features and APIs for defining flexible and responsive layouts, including support for flex containers, flex items, alignment, spacing, and wrapping. By using these libraries, developers can easily create complex UI designs that automatically adjust to the available space and accommodate changes in content or screen size.

One of the key concepts in Flexbox layout is the notion of flex containers and flex items. A flex container is a container component that uses Flexbox layout to organize its child components, known as flex items, along a flex direction, which can be horizontal or vertical. Flex items can have flexible or fixed dimensions, allowing them to grow or shrink dynamically based on available space and content constraints. This flexibility enables developers to create fluid and adaptive layouts that adapt gracefully to different screen sizes and resolutions.

In addition to flex containers and flex items, Flexbox layout introduces a set of powerful alignment and spacing properties that enable precise control over the positioning and sizing of components within a layout. These properties include justifyContent, alignItems, alignSelf, alignContent, flexWrap, flexFlow, and flex. By using these properties, developers can specify how flex items are aligned, spaced, wrapped, and resized within a flex container, ensuring consistent and visually appealing layouts across different devices and platforms.

To illustrate the use of Flexbox layout in Java Swing, let's consider an example where we have a JPanel as a flex container containing multiple JLabels as flex items. We can use a FlexLayout manager to define the layout of the JPanel and specify the alignment, spacing, and wrapping properties to achieve the desired layout. For instance, we can set the flex direction to horizontal, justify the content to the center, align items to the center, and wrap items when they exceed the available width. This configuration ensures that the JLabels are evenly spaced, centered, and wrapped as needed, providing a responsive and visually appealing layout.

javaCopy code

```
import javax.swing.*; import com.miglayout.swing.MigLayout; public class FlexboxExample { public static void main(String[] args) { JFrame frame = new JFrame("Flexbox Layout Example"); JPanel panel = new JPanel(new MigLayout("wrap 3", "[grow]", "[grow]")); // Create and add JLabels as flex items for (int i = 1; i <= 6; i++) { JLabel label = new JLabel("Label " + i); panel.add(label, "grow, wmin 100, hmin 100"); // Flex item with minimum size } frame.add(panel); frame.setDefaultCloseOperation(JFrame.EXIT_ON_CLOSE); frame.setSize(400, 300); frame.setLocationRelativeTo(null); frame.setVisible(true); } }
```

In this example, we create a JFrame with a JPanel using MigLayout as the layout manager. We specify "wrap 3" to indicate that the layout should wrap items into multiple rows with a maximum of three items per row. Additionally, we use the "grow" constraint to allow the JLabels to expand to fill the available space within the flex container. Finally, we set minimum width and height constraints to ensure that the JLabels have a minimum size to prevent them from becoming too small when resized.

By using Flexbox layout in Java Swing, developers can create modern and responsive user interfaces that adapt dynamically to different screen sizes and orientations, offering a consistent and intuitive user experience across various devices and platforms. With its flexible and powerful layout model, Flexbox layout revolutionizes UI design in Swing applications, enabling developers to build sophisticated and visually appealing interfaces that meet the demands of today's diverse and dynamic digital landscape.

Responsive design strategies for Swing applications are essential for creating user interfaces that adapt seamlessly to different screen sizes, resolutions, and orientations, providing users with a consistent and optimal viewing experience across various devices and platforms. Unlike web development, where responsive design is commonly associated with CSS media queries and flexible layouts, implementing responsive design in Swing applications requires a different approach due to Swing's desktop-centric nature. However, with careful planning and the right techniques, developers can achieve responsive UIs in Swing applications that meet the expectations of modern users.

One effective strategy for responsive design in Swing applications is to use layout managers that support dynamic resizing and component repositioning, such as GroupLayout or MigLayout. These layout managers allow developers to define flexible and adaptive layouts that adjust automatically to changes in screen size or content, ensuring that UI elements are properly positioned and sized across different devices and resolutions. By leveraging the capabilities of these layout managers, developers can create UIs that scale gracefully from desktop monitors to smaller screens like laptops or tablets, without sacrificing usability or readability.

Another important aspect of responsive design in Swing applications is optimizing the use of whitespace and arranging UI elements in a visually pleasing and logical manner. This involves prioritizing content based on importance and relevance, using appropriate spacing and alignment to improve readability, and avoiding cluttered or overcrowded layouts that can overwhelm users. By carefully designing the layout and organization of UI elements, developers can create UIs that are both aesthetically pleasing and easy to navigate, regardless of the device or screen size.

Furthermore, responsive design in Swing applications involves adapting UI behavior and interaction patterns to suit different input methods and device capabilities. For example, developers can implement touch-friendly controls and gestures for touchscreen devices, provide keyboard shortcuts and accelerators for desktop users, and ensure that UI elements are accessible and usable with assistive technologies such as screen readers or voice commands. By considering the diverse needs and preferences of users, developers can create responsive UIs that are inclusive and accessible to all.

Additionally, responsive design in Swing applications encompasses optimizing performance and resource usage to ensure smooth and efficient operation across different devices and platforms. This involves minimizing unnecessary UI updates, optimizing the rendering and layout process, and leveraging hardware acceleration and caching techniques where applicable. By optimizing performance, developers can create responsive UIs that deliver a fluid and responsive user experience, even on lower-powered devices or in resource-constrained environments.

Another important consideration for responsive design in Swing applications is supporting localization and internationalization to accommodate users from different regions and cultures. This involves designing UIs that can adapt to different languages, character sets, and text directions, as well as providing culturally appropriate content and imagery. By implementing proper localization and internationalization practices, developers can ensure that their Swing applications are accessible and usable by a global audience, regardless of language or cultural background.

Furthermore, responsive design in Swing applications involves testing and validating UIs across a diverse range of devices, screen sizes, and operating systems to ensure compatibility and consistency. This includes conducting usability testing with real users to identify and address any usability issues or pain points, as well as leveraging automated testing tools and frameworks to detect and fix layout or rendering problems. By thoroughly testing and validating UIs, developers can ensure that their Swing applications deliver a seamless and intuitive user experience across all target platforms.

In summary, responsive design strategies for Swing applications are essential for creating user interfaces that adapt gracefully to different devices, screen sizes, and user preferences. By leveraging flexible layout managers, optimizing whitespace and organization, adapting UI behavior and interaction patterns, optimizing performance and resource usage, supporting localization and internationalization, and testing across diverse environments, developers can create responsive UIs that meet the needs of modern users and provide a consistent and optimal viewing experience across all platforms.

**Chapter 5: Working with Swing Models and Renderers**

Customizing table models for complex data is a crucial aspect of developing Swing applications, particularly when dealing with large datasets or hierarchical data structures. Swing provides the JTable component for displaying tabular data, but to effectively manage and display complex data, developers often need to customize the underlying table model. The table model serves as the data source for the JTable, defining how data is organized, accessed, and displayed within the table. By customizing the table model, developers can implement advanced features such as sorting, filtering, grouping, and editing, tailored to the specific requirements of their application.

One common approach to customizing table models for complex data is to subclass AbstractTableModel, a convenient abstract implementation of the TableModel interface provided by Swing. By extending AbstractTableModel, developers can define custom methods for accessing and manipulating the underlying data structure, such as adding or removing rows, updating cell values, or retrieving data based on specific criteria. Additionally, developers can override methods like getValueAt(), setValueAt(), getRowCount(), and getColumnCount() to provide custom implementations that reflect the structure and content of their data.

Another important aspect of customizing table models for complex data is implementing support for sorting and filtering. Swing does not provide built-in support for sorting or filtering data in JTable components, so developers must implement these features themselves within the custom table model. One common approach is to maintain separate data structures for the original unsorted data and the sorted or filtered data, updating the table model accordingly based on user interactions or external events. By implementing sorting and filtering functionality within the table model, developers can provide users with powerful tools for organizing and navigating large datasets efficiently.

Furthermore, customizing table models for complex data often involves implementing support for hierarchical or nested data structures. While JTable is primarily designed for displaying flat tabular data, developers can leverage custom table models to represent hierarchical relationships between data elements, such as parent-child or master-detail relationships. One approach is to subclass DefaultTreeTableModel, an extension of AbstractTableModel that provides support for displaying hierarchical data in a tree-like structure. By implementing custom methods for traversing and accessing hierarchical data, developers can create rich and interactive user interfaces that visualize complex data relationships effectively.

In addition to supporting sorting, filtering, and hierarchical data structures, customizing table models for complex data may also involve implementing support for advanced editing and validation. Swing provides built-in support for basic cell editing using editors and renderers, but for more complex editing scenarios, developers may need to implement custom editors and validators tailored to their application's specific requirements. By subclassing TableCellEditor and TableCellRenderer interfaces, developers can create custom components for editing and rendering cell values, providing users with a seamless and intuitive editing experience.

Moreover, customizing table models for complex data often requires optimizing performance and resource usage, particularly when dealing with large datasets or frequent updates. To improve performance, developers can implement techniques such as lazy loading, where data is loaded into memory only when needed, or caching, where frequently accessed data is cached for faster retrieval. Additionally, developers can leverage multithreading and background processing to offload intensive data processing tasks from the event dispatch thread, ensuring that the UI remains responsive and fluid even when handling large amounts of data.

Furthermore, customizing table models for complex data may involve implementing support for data validation and error handling. Swing does not provide built-in support for data validation in JTable components, so developers must implement custom validation logic within the table model to enforce data integrity and consistency. By implementing custom validation methods and error handling mechanisms, developers can ensure that invalid data is not allowed to be entered or displayed in the table, maintaining the integrity and reliability of the application's data.

Additionally, customizing table models for complex data may involve implementing support for dynamic updates and real-time synchronization with external data sources. In modern applications, data is often dynamic and continuously updated, requiring the UI to reflect changes in real-time. To achieve this, developers can implement techniques such as event-driven updates, where the table model listens for events or notifications from external data sources and updates the UI accordingly. By implementing dynamic update mechanisms within the table model, developers can create responsive and interactive user interfaces that reflect the latest changes in the underlying data.

In summary, customizing table models for complex data is a fundamental aspect of developing Swing applications that require advanced data management and visualization capabilities. By subclassing AbstractTableModel, implementing support for sorting, filtering, and hierarchical data structures, optimizing performance and resource usage, implementing advanced editing and validation, and supporting dynamic updates and real-time synchronization, developers can create powerful and flexible table models that meet the specific requirements of their application, providing users with a rich and interactive data browsing experience. Implementing custom cell renderers and editors is a crucial aspect of developing Swing applications that require advanced and customized UI components for displaying and editing tabular data. In Swing, JTable components are commonly used for presenting tabular data, and cell renderers and editors define how data is visualized and manipulated within individual table cells. By customizing cell renderers and editors, developers can enhance the appearance and functionality of JTable components, providing users with a more intuitive and efficient data browsing and editing experience.

One approach to implementing custom cell renderers and editors in Swing is to subclass DefaultTableCellRenderer and DefaultCellEditor, which are provided by Swing as default implementations of the TableCellRenderer and TableCellEditor interfaces, respectively. By extending these classes, developers can define custom rendering and editing behavior for specific data types or application requirements. For example, a custom cell renderer may display numeric data with a specific format or color scheme, while a custom cell editor may provide specialized input controls for editing date or time values.

Another important aspect of implementing custom cell renderers and editors is defining how data is rendered and edited within individual table cells. Cell renderers are responsible for painting the visual representation of cell content, while cell editors are responsible for providing input controls and handling user interactions for editing cell values. By overriding the getTableCellRendererComponent() method in a custom cell renderer, developers can customize how cell content is displayed, such as applying custom formatting, applying conditional styling based on cell values, or incorporating custom graphics or icons.

Similarly, by overriding the getTableCellEditorComponent() method in a custom cell editor, developers can define the input controls and user interface elements used for editing cell values. For example, a custom cell editor for editing numeric values may use a formatted text field with validation logic to ensure that only valid numeric input is accepted, while a custom cell editor for editing text values may use a multi-line text area with support for syntax highlighting or code completion. Furthermore, implementing custom cell renderers and editors often involves managing the state and behavior of individual table cells, such as handling selection, focus, and keyboard navigation. By overriding methods such as isCellEditable(), shouldSelectCell(), and getTableCellEditorComponent(), developers can control when and how cell editing is initiated, as well as handle any additional interactions or events that occur during editing. Additionally, developers can implement custom event listeners or event handlers to respond to user actions such as mouse clicks, key presses, or focus changes within individual table cells. Moreover, implementing custom cell renderers and editors may involve optimizing performance and resource usage, particularly when dealing with large datasets or complex rendering requirements. To improve performance, developers can implement techniques such as cell caching, where previously rendered cell contents are reused to avoid unnecessary rendering operations, or cell pooling, where a limited number of renderer or editor instances are reused to reduce memory overhead. Additionally, developers can leverage asynchronous rendering or lazy loading techniques to defer rendering or editing operations until they are needed, ensuring that the UI remains responsive and fluid even when handling large amounts of data. Additionally, implementing custom cell renderers and editors often involves testing and validation to ensure that they behave correctly and consistently across different platforms and environments. Developers can use unit testing frameworks such as JUnit to test individual renderer and editor implementations, as well as integration testing tools to validate their behavior within the context of a complete Swing application. By thoroughly testing and validating custom cell renderers and editors, developers can ensure that they meet the functional and performance requirements of their application, providing users with a seamless and intuitive data browsing and editing experience.

In summary, implementing custom cell renderers and editors is a fundamental aspect of developing Swing applications that require advanced and customized UI components for displaying and editing tabular data. By subclassing DefaultTableCellRenderer and DefaultCellEditor, defining custom rendering and editing behavior, managing cell state and behavior, optimizing performance and resource usage, and testing and validating implementations, developers can create powerful and flexible cell renderers and editors that meet the specific requirements of their application, providing users with a rich and interactive data browsing and editing experience.

## Chapter 6: Creating Custom Swing Components

Extending Swing components for specialized functionality is a pivotal aspect of developing rich and tailored user interfaces in Java applications. Swing, being a comprehensive GUI toolkit, provides a wide array of components for building interactive applications, but often developers need to extend these components to meet specific requirements or to introduce new features. By subclassing existing Swing components and augmenting them with custom functionality, developers can create highly specialized and versatile UI elements that cater to the unique needs of their applications.

One of the primary motivations for extending Swing components is to add specialized behavior or appearance that goes beyond the standard capabilities provided by the core set of components. For example, developers may need to create custom buttons with unique visual styles or interactive behaviors, such as animated icons or complex tooltip interactions. By subclassing JButton and overriding methods like paintComponent() or actionPerformed(), developers can implement custom rendering and event handling logic to achieve the desired functionality while maintaining compatibility with existing Swing APIs.

Moreover, extending Swing components allows developers to encapsulate complex functionality into reusable and modular units, promoting code reusability and maintainability across different parts of the application. For instance, developers may create custom components for displaying specialized data visualizations, such as charts, graphs, or diagrams, that can be easily integrated into various parts of the application's UI. By encapsulating the rendering and interaction logic within custom component classes, developers can abstract away the complexity of the underlying implementation and provide a clean and intuitive interface for interacting with the data.

Furthermore, extending Swing components enables developers to introduce advanced or experimental features that are not available in the standard Swing library. For example, developers may create custom text input components with support for advanced text editing features, such as syntax highlighting, code completion, or spell checking. By subclassing JTextComponent and implementing custom caret, document, and key event handling logic, developers can create powerful text editing components that offer enhanced productivity and usability for users.

Additionally, extending Swing components facilitates the implementation of complex UI patterns or design paradigms that are specific to the application domain or user experience requirements. For instance, developers may create custom components for implementing wizard dialogs, tree-table views, or drag-and-drop interfaces, each tailored to the unique interaction patterns and workflows of the application. By subclassing existing Swing components or combining multiple components into composite structures, developers can create rich and intuitive user interfaces that seamlessly integrate with the overall application design.

Moreover, extending Swing components allows developers to address performance or scalability limitations inherent in the standard Swing library. For example, developers may create custom components optimized for rendering large datasets or handling complex data structures efficiently. By implementing custom rendering algorithms, data caching strategies, or asynchronous processing mechanisms, developers can create high-performance components that deliver responsive and fluid user experiences even when dealing with large amounts of data.

Furthermore, extending Swing components enables developers to integrate third-party libraries or technologies seamlessly into Swing-based applications. For example, developers may create custom components for embedding web content using browser rendering engines like Chromium or WebKit, or for integrating multimedia content using media frameworks like JavaFX or VLCJ. By leveraging the flexibility and extensibility of Swing's component model, developers can create hybrid applications that combine the strengths of different technologies to deliver rich and immersive user experiences.

In summary, extending Swing components for specialized functionality is a powerful technique for building rich and tailored user interfaces in Java applications. By subclassing existing Swing components, encapsulating complex functionality into reusable units, introducing advanced features or experimental concepts, implementing complex UI patterns or design paradigms, addressing performance or scalability limitations, and integrating third-party libraries or technologies, developers can create highly specialized and versatile UI elements that meet the specific requirements of their applications, providing users with intuitive, efficient, and engaging user experiences.

Building composite components with custom behaviors is a fundamental aspect of GUI development, especially in Java Swing applications, where developers often need to create complex user interface elements that combine multiple components with specialized interactions and functionality. Composite components are comprised of multiple subcomponents arranged in a specific layout to form a cohesive unit, and they play a crucial role in creating intuitive and user-friendly interfaces. By combining existing Swing components and implementing custom behaviors, developers can create powerful and flexible composite components that meet the unique requirements of their applications.

To build composite components with custom behaviors in Swing, developers typically start by identifying the specific functionality and interactions required by the component. This involves analyzing the user interface requirements and determining which existing Swing components can be combined to achieve the desired functionality. For example, developers may need to create a composite component for displaying a custom data entry form with input fields, labels, buttons, and validation logic.

Once the requirements are clear, developers can begin designing the layout and structure of the composite component. This involves selecting an appropriate layout manager, such as BorderLayout, GridLayout, or GroupLayout, to arrange the subcomponents within the composite component. The layout manager determines how the subcomponents are positioned and sized relative to each other, ensuring that the composite component appears visually coherent and aligns with the overall design of the application.

Next, developers proceed to assemble the composite component by adding the necessary subcomponents and configuring their properties and behaviors. This may involve instantiating instances of existing Swing components, such as JLabel, JTextField, JButton, or JCheckBox, and setting their properties, such as text, icon, tooltip, or event handlers. Additionally, developers may need to customize the appearance or behavior of individual subcomponents to meet specific requirements, such as applying custom styling, adding event listeners, or implementing specialized functionality.

One common approach to implementing custom behaviors in composite components is to subclass existing Swing components and override their methods to provide the desired functionality. For example, developers may subclass JButton to create a custom button component with a specialized appearance or behavior, such as an animated icon or a tooltip that displays additional information when hovered over. Similarly, developers may subclass JTextField to create a custom text input field with validation logic or auto-completion features.

Another approach to implementing custom behaviors in composite components is to encapsulate the behavior within dedicated event listeners or action handlers. For example, developers may attach action listeners to buttons or text fields to handle user interactions, such as button clicks or text input events. By encapsulating the behavior within event listeners, developers can decouple the logic from the individual components, making the composite component more modular and easier to maintain.

Additionally, developers may leverage the Model-View-Controller (MVC) design pattern to separate the presentation, data, and control logic of composite components. In this approach, the model represents the data or state of the component, the view represents the visual presentation of the component, and the controller mediates user interactions and updates the model accordingly. By organizing the code according to the MVC pattern, developers can achieve better separation of concerns and improve the maintainability and scalability of composite components.

Furthermore, building composite components with custom behaviors often involves implementing support for user interactions and feedback mechanisms, such as keyboard shortcuts, mouse gestures, or tooltips. For example, developers may implement keyboard shortcuts to trigger specific actions within the composite component, or they may use mouse listeners to detect mouse gestures and provide visual feedback to the user. Additionally, developers may incorporate tooltips to provide contextual information or guidance to users when interacting with the component.

Moreover, developers may need to consider accessibility requirements when building composite components with custom behaviors. This involves ensuring that the component is usable and navigable by users with disabilities, such as providing keyboard navigation support, ensuring proper focus management, and implementing accessible labels and descriptions. By adhering to accessibility guidelines and best practices, developers can ensure that the composite component is inclusive and accessible to all users.

In summary, building composite components with custom behaviors is a core aspect of GUI development in Java Swing applications. By combining existing Swing components, implementing custom behaviors, designing layouts, and considering usability and accessibility requirements, developers can create powerful and versatile composite components that enhance the user experience and meet the unique requirements of their applications. Through careful design and implementation, composite components can serve as building blocks for creating intuitive, feature-rich, and visually appealing user interfaces in Swing applications.

# Chapter 7: Data Binding and Validation in Swing

Binding data to Swing components with bean binding is a powerful technique that facilitates the synchronization of data between Java objects and user interface elements in Swing applications. Bean binding allows developers to establish a bidirectional relationship between properties of JavaBeans and properties of Swing components, enabling automatic updates of the UI when the underlying data changes, and vice versa. This technique streamlines the development process, reduces boilerplate code, and enhances the maintainability of Swing applications by promoting a separation of concerns between the presentation layer and the data model.

The process of binding data to Swing components typically involves three main steps: defining the data model, configuring the binding, and updating the UI. Firstly, developers define the data model using JavaBeans, which are Java classes that adhere to the JavaBeans specification and encapsulate the application's data. Each property of the JavaBean represents a piece of data that needs to be displayed or manipulated in the UI. For example, in a simple address book application, the data model might include properties such as name, email, and phone number.

Once the data model is defined, developers configure the binding between the properties of the JavaBeans and the properties of the Swing components. This is achieved using a binding framework, such as Beans Binding (JSR 295) or Glazed Lists, which provides APIs for establishing and managing the bindings. The binding framework typically allows developers to specify the source and target properties, as well as any conversion or validation logic that needs to be applied. For example, developers can bind the text property of a JTextField to the name property of a JavaBean, ensuring that any changes to the name property are automatically reflected in the text field.

To configure the binding, developers use the relevant APIs provided by the binding framework. For example, in Beans Binding, developers use the Bindings class to create bindings between properties. The Bindings class provides static methods for creating different types of bindings, such as binding properties of Swing components to properties of JavaBeans, binding collections to list or table components, or binding custom converters and validators. Developers can use these methods to configure the bindings according to their specific requirements.

Once the bindings are configured, the data is automatically synchronized between the JavaBeans and the Swing components. This means that changes to the properties of the JavaBeans are immediately reflected in the UI, and changes made by the user in the UI are propagated back to the JavaBeans. For example, if the user edits the text in a JTextField, the corresponding property of the JavaBean is updated automatically, and any other bound components that display the same property are also updated accordingly.

Bean binding offers several benefits for Swing application development. Firstly, it simplifies the code by eliminating the need for manual event handling and synchronization logic. Instead of writing boilerplate code to update the UI in response to changes in the data model, developers can rely on the binding framework to handle these tasks automatically. This reduces the amount of code that needs to be written and makes the codebase more concise and maintainable.

Secondly, bean binding promotes a separation of concerns between the presentation layer and the data model. By binding Swing components directly to properties of JavaBeans, developers can encapsulate the data model logic within the JavaBeans and keep the presentation logic separate. This makes the codebase easier to understand, test, and maintain, as each component is responsible for a specific aspect of the application's functionality.

Thirdly, bean binding improves the responsiveness and usability of Swing applications by ensuring that the UI is always up-to-date with the underlying data. Users can interact with the UI in real-time, confident that any changes they make will be immediately reflected in the data model, and vice versa. This enhances the overall user experience and makes the application more intuitive and user-friendly.

Moreover, bean binding provides support for complex data structures and relationships, such as nested properties, collections, and master-detail views. Developers can easily bind nested properties of

JavaBeans to nested components in the UI, or bind collections of data to list or table components for display. This allows developers to build sophisticated and dynamic user interfaces that can adapt to a wide range of data scenarios.

In summary, binding data to Swing components with bean binding is a powerful technique that simplifies the development of Swing applications, enhances code maintainability, and improves the user experience. By establishing a bidirectional relationship between properties of JavaBeans and properties of Swing components, developers can create responsive, intuitive, and feature-rich user interfaces that seamlessly synchronize with the underlying data model. Through the use of binding frameworks such as Beans Binding or Glazed Lists, developers can streamline the development process and focus on building robust and scalable applications that meet the needs of their users.

Implementing input validation for Swing forms is a critical aspect of developing robust and user-friendly applications. Input validation ensures that the data entered by users is accurate, consistent, and conforms to the expected format, preventing errors and enhancing the overall user experience. By validating user input at the point of entry, developers can detect and handle errors early, reducing the likelihood of data corruption and improving data integrity.

One common approach to implementing input validation in Swing forms is to use input verifiers, which are components that validate user input as it is entered into text fields or other input components. Input verifiers allow developers to define custom validation logic for each input field, specifying the criteria that the input must meet in order to be considered valid. For example, developers can validate text fields to ensure that they contain only alphanumeric characters, or that they are within a certain range of values.

To implement input validation using input verifiers, developers typically create a subclass of javax.swing.InputVerifier and override its shouldYieldFocus method. This method is called whenever the focus is about to move from one component to another, allowing the input verifier to perform validation checks on the current component's input. If the input is deemed invalid, the shouldYieldFocus method returns false, preventing the focus from moving to the next component and indicating to the user that there is an error in the input.

For example, suppose we have a text field that is supposed to accept only numeric input. We can create a custom input verifier for this text field by subclassing InputVerifier and implementing the shouldYieldFocus method to validate the input. If the input is not numeric, we can display an error message to the user and prevent the focus from moving to the next component until the input is corrected.

javaCopy code

```
import javax.swing.InputVerifier; import javax.swing.JComponent; import javax.swing.JTextField; public class NumericInputVerifier extends InputVerifier {
```

```
@Override public boolean shouldYieldFocus(JComponent input) { JTextField textField = (JTextField) input; String text = textField.getText(); // Validate input if (!text.matches("\\d+")) { // Display error message textField.setText("");
textField.requestFocusInWindow(); // Return false to indicate invalid input return false; } // Return true to indicate valid input return true; } }
```

Once the input verifier is defined, developers can attach it to the relevant input components using the setInputVerifier method. This associates the input verifier with the input component, causing it to be invoked whenever the focus moves to or from the component. By attaching input verifiers to all relevant input components in a form, developers can ensure that user input is validated consistently and comprehensively across the entire form.

javaCopy code

```
JTextField numericField = new JTextField(); numericField.setInputVerifier(new
NumericInputVerifier());
```

In addition to input verifiers, Swing forms can also benefit from the use of formatted text fields, which enforce specific input formats such as dates, phone numbers, or currency amounts. Formatted text fields allow developers to specify a format mask that defines the allowed input format and automatically validates user input against this format. For example, developers can use a MaskFormatter to create a formatted text field that only accepts numeric input in a specific format, such as a phone number with parentheses around the area code.

javaCopy code

```
import javax.swing.JFormattedTextField; import javax.swing.text.MaskFormatter; try { MaskFormatter formatter = new MaskFormatter("(###) ###-####"); JFormattedTextField phoneField = new JFormattedTextField(formatter); } catch (ParseException e) { e.printStackTrace(); }
```

Formatted text fields provide a convenient way to enforce input validation for complex data formats, reducing the likelihood of user input errors and improving the accuracy and reliability of the application's data. However, it's important to note that formatted text fields have limitations in terms of flexibility and customization compared to input verifiers, so developers should choose the appropriate validation technique based on the specific requirements of their application.

In addition to input verifiers and formatted text fields, Swing forms can also incorporate error feedback mechanisms to provide users with clear and actionable feedback when validation errors occur. This can include displaying error messages next to invalid input fields, highlighting the fields in red, or using tooltips to explain the validation requirements. By providing immediate feedback to users, developers can help them quickly identify and correct input errors, leading to a more efficient and frustration-free user experience.

Overall, implementing input validation for Swing forms is essential for ensuring data accuracy, integrity, and usability in desktop applications. By using input verifiers, formatted text fields, and error feedback mechanisms, developers can create forms that guide users towards correct input, prevent data entry errors, and enhance the overall quality of the application. With careful planning and attention to detail, developers can design forms that are intuitive, user-friendly, and reliable, resulting in a positive and productive user experience.

## Chapter 8: Multithreading and Concurrency in Swing Applications

Understanding Swing's single-threaded model is crucial for developing robust and responsive Java GUI applications. In Swing, all UI-related operations must be performed on the Event Dispatch Thread (EDT) to ensure thread safety and prevent concurrency issues. This single-threaded approach simplifies the development process by eliminating the need for manual synchronization but also requires careful attention to avoid performance bottlenecks and unresponsiveness in the UI. To adhere to Swing's single-threaded model, developers must understand how Swing manages threads, how to execute tasks on the EDT, and how to handle long-running operations without blocking the UI.

Swing's single-threaded model revolves around the Event Dispatch Thread (EDT), which is responsible for processing user events, updating the UI, and executing event-handling code. All UI-related operations, such as creating or modifying Swing components, handling user input, and updating component properties, must be performed on the EDT to maintain consistency and prevent data corruption. The EDT ensures thread safety by serializing event dispatching and executing tasks sequentially, thereby avoiding race conditions and other concurrency issues.

To execute tasks on the EDT, developers can utilize SwingUtilities.invokeLater() or SwingUtilities.invokeAndWait(). These utility methods enqueue tasks onto the EDT's event queue, ensuring that they are executed in a thread-safe manner. For example, to update a Swing component's properties from a non-EDT thread, developers can wrap the modification code inside a Runnable and pass it to invokeLater() or invokeAndWait(), ensuring that the changes are applied on the EDT.

It's essential to note that long-running or blocking operations should not be executed on the EDT, as they can cause the UI to become unresponsive. Instead, such tasks should be offloaded to worker threads to prevent blocking the EDT. Swing provides the SwingWorker class, which facilitates the execution of background tasks while allowing updates to the UI on the EDT. By using SwingWorker, developers can perform tasks such as file I/O, network communication, or heavy computation without freezing the UI.

In addition to SwingWorker, developers can leverage other concurrency utilities provided by Java, such as Executors and Callable, to execute tasks concurrently and asynchronously. For example, developers can create a ThreadPoolExecutor to manage a pool of worker threads and submit tasks for execution. By separating long-running operations from the EDT, developers can ensure that the UI remains responsive and maintains a smooth user experience.

Furthermore, Swing's single-threaded model has implications for handling events and event listeners.

Event listeners are executed on the EDT when triggered by user actions or system events. It's crucial to keep event-handling code lightweight and responsive to prevent blocking the EDT. Long-running event-handling tasks should be delegated to worker threads to avoid delaying event processing and UI updates.

Another aspect of Swing's single-threaded model is the use of timers for scheduling and executing periodic tasks. Swing provides the javax.swing.Timer class, which allows developers to schedule tasks to be executed at regular intervals on the EDT. By using timers, developers can implement features such as animations, periodic updates, or automatic refreshes without blocking the EDT or causing UI stuttering.

Overall, understanding Swing's single-threaded model is essential for developing efficient and responsive GUI applications in Java. By adhering to Swing's threading rules, leveraging concurrency utilities, and offloading long-running tasks to worker threads, developers can create applications that provide a smooth and seamless user experience. It's crucial to keep the EDT free from blocking operations and ensure that UI updates and event handling are performed efficiently to maintain the responsiveness and usability of Swing applications.

Accessing Swing components from multiple threads introduces complexities and challenges due to Swing's single-threaded model, where all UI-related operations must occur on the Event Dispatch Thread (EDT) to ensure thread safety. Violating this rule can lead to race conditions, deadlock, and other concurrency issues.

However, there are techniques and best practices developers can employ to safely interact with Swing components from multiple threads.

One common approach is to use SwingUtilities.invokeLater() or SwingUtilities.invokeAndWait() to execute code on the EDT from non-EDT threads. These utility methods enqueue tasks onto the EDT's event queue, ensuring that UI-related operations are performed sequentially and in a thread-safe manner. For example, to update a Swing component's properties from a background thread, developers can wrap the modification code inside a Runnable and pass it to invokeLater() or invokeAndWait(), guaranteeing that the changes are applied on the EDT.

Another technique is to leverage SwingWorker for asynchronous background tasks that involve Swing components. SwingWorker allows developers to perform long-running operations off the EDT while still being able to update the UI safely. By overriding the doInBackground() method to perform the background task and the done() method to update the UI with the results, developers can ensure that Swing components are accessed only on the EDT, preventing concurrency issues.

Additionally, developers can use the EventQueue.invokeLater() method to post tasks directly to the EDT's event queue. While similar to SwingUtilities.invokeLater(), this method provides a more low-level approach for enqueuing tasks onto the EDT. However, it's essential to note that

EventQueue.invokeLater() should be used cautiously, as it doesn't handle exceptions or synchronization automatically like SwingUtilities.invokeLater() does.

Furthermore, developers should be aware of Swing's concurrency policies when interacting with components from multiple threads. For instance, modifying Swing components' properties directly from non-EDT threads can lead to unpredictable behavior and potential UI corruption. Instead, developers should use EDT-safe methods such as SwingUtilities.invokeLater() or invokeAndWait() to update Swing components safely.

Another consideration is avoiding excessive locking or synchronization when accessing Swing components from multiple threads. While it's essential to ensure thread safety, excessive locking can lead to performance bottlenecks and potential deadlocks. Developers should aim to minimize the use of synchronized blocks and locks when accessing Swing components concurrently.

Moreover, developers should be cautious when sharing mutable data between threads that interact with Swing components. Immutable or thread-safe data structures should be preferred to avoid data corruption or synchronization issues. Additionally, developers should use thread-safe Swing components such as JList, JTable, and JTextArea when possible, as these components handle concurrency internally.

In summary, safely accessing Swing components from multiple threads requires adherence to Swing's single-threaded model and the use of appropriate concurrency techniques. By leveraging utilities like

SwingUtilities.invokeLater(), SwingWorker, and EventQueue.invokeLater(), developers can ensure that UI-related operations are performed safely and efficiently across multiple threads. Additionally, minimizing locking and synchronization and using thread-safe Swing components can help mitigate concurrency issues and ensure a smooth user experience in Swing applications.

## Chapter 9: Implementing Drag-and-Drop Reordering

Enabling drag-and-drop functionality between Swing components enhances user interaction and workflow in Java GUI applications, allowing users to intuitively manipulate data and objects. Implementing drag-and-drop functionality involves several steps, including setting up drag sources, drop targets, and handling drag-and-drop events.

To enable drag-and-drop functionality in a Swing application, developers first need to designate components as drag sources and drop targets. For drag sources, such as JList, JTree, or JTable, developers can use built-in methods like setDragEnabled(true) to enable dragging. Similarly, drop targets, where data can be dropped, need to be designated using setDropTarget().

Once the drag sources and drop targets are established, developers need to define the behavior of the drag-and-drop operation. This involves handling various drag-and-drop events, such as drag started, drag entered, drag exited, and drop completed. Swing provides a set of listener interfaces, such as DragGestureListener, DragSourceListener, and DropTargetListener, to handle these events and customize the drag-and-drop behavior.

For example, to initiate a drag operation, developers can implement the DragGestureListener interface and override its methods to start the drag when a user initiates a drag gesture. Within these methods, developers can specify the drag source, drag actions, and transferable data to be transferred during the drag operation.

Similarly, to handle drop events, developers need to implement the DropTargetListener interface and override its methods to handle drop-related events such as drag enter, drag exit, drag over, and drop. Within these methods, developers can specify the behavior when a drop occurs, such as accepting or rejecting the dropped data, and perform any necessary data processing or manipulation.

Additionally, developers can customize the appearance and behavior of drag-and-drop operations by providing custom drag images, feedback, and cursor icons. This can be achieved by implementing custom TransferHandler subclasses for drag sources and drop targets and overriding their methods to customize the appearance and behavior of the drag-and-drop operation.

Moreover, developers should consider accessibility and usability aspects when implementing drag-and-drop functionality. Providing clear visual feedback, keyboard support, and appropriate drag-and-drop hints can enhance the user experience and ensure accessibility for users with disabilities.

In terms of deployment, enabling drag-and-drop functionality in a Swing application typically involves writing code to handle drag-and-drop events and registering drag-and-drop listeners with drag sources and drop targets. The application can then be compiled and executed using Java development tools such as javac and java from the command line or integrated development environments (IDEs) like Eclipse or IntelliJ IDEA.

Overall, enabling drag-and-drop functionality between Swing components enhances the usability and interactivity of Java GUI applications. By following the steps outlined above and customizing drag-and-drop behavior to suit the application's requirements, developers can create intuitive and user-friendly interfaces that empower users to efficiently manipulate data and objects within the application.

Customizing drag-and-drop behavior for different data types in Swing applications is a crucial aspect of enhancing user experience and functionality. By tailoring the drag-and-drop behavior to specific data types, developers can provide users with more intuitive and efficient ways to interact with data. This customization involves defining how different types of data are represented during drag-and-drop operations, specifying which data types can be dragged and dropped, and implementing logic to handle the conversion between different data formats.

At the core of customizing drag-and-drop behavior for different data types is the TransferHandler class in Swing. TransferHandler provides a flexible framework for defining how data is transferred between drag sources and drop targets. Developers can subclass TransferHandler to customize the behavior for specific data types and override methods such as createTransferable(), importData(), and exportDone() to implement custom drag-and-drop logic.

One common scenario for customizing drag-and-drop behavior is when dealing with complex data structures or objects that need to be serialized and deserialized during drag-and-drop operations. For example, in a file management application, developers may want to allow users to drag files from one location to another within the application. In this case, the TransferHandler subclass would need to implement logic to serialize the file data into a transferable format during drag operations and deserialize it back into file objects during drop operations.

To implement this behavior, developers can override the createTransferable() method of TransferHandler to create a Transferable object that encapsulates the data being dragged. This could involve serializing the file data into a byte array or another suitable format that can be transferred between components. Once the drag operation is initiated, the TransferHandler's exportDone() method can be used to clean up any resources used during the drag operation.

Similarly, on the drop side, developers need to implement logic to handle the incoming data and convert it back into the appropriate format for use within the application. This typically involves overriding the importData() method of TransferHandler and extracting the data from the Transferable object passed as a parameter. Developers can then deserialize the data and perform any necessary processing to integrate it into the application.

Another aspect of customizing drag-and-drop behavior for different data types is specifying which data types can be dragged and dropped and defining the visual feedback provided to users during drag operations. Swing provides mechanisms for specifying the supported data flavors and customizing the drag-and-drop feedback using the TransferHandler class.

For instance, developers can override the getSourceActions() method of TransferHandler to specify the drag actions supported by a drag source component, such as COPY, MOVE, or LINK. They can also customize the appearance of the drag image and cursor using the setDragImage() and setDragCursor() methods of TransferHandler to provide visual feedback to users during drag operations.

In terms of deployment, customizing drag-and-drop behavior for different data types in Swing applications involves implementing and registering TransferHandler subclasses with drag sources and drop targets. This can typically be done within the application's codebase using a Java development environment such as IntelliJ IDEA or Eclipse. Once implemented, the application can be compiled and executed using the Java compiler and runtime environment.

In summary, customizing drag-and-drop behavior for different data types in Swing applications is essential for providing users with intuitive and efficient ways to interact with data. By subclassing TransferHandler and implementing custom logic for serializing, deserializing, and handling different data formats, developers can tailor the drag-and-drop experience to suit the application's requirements. Additionally, specifying supported drag actions and customizing drag feedback enhances the usability and visual appeal of the application.

## Chapter 10: Integrating JavaFX Components into Swing Applications

Embedding JavaFX components in Swing applications is a powerful technique that allows developers to leverage the rich features and capabilities of JavaFX within their Swing-based user interfaces. This integration enables developers to create modern and visually appealing user interfaces while maintaining compatibility with existing Swing codebases.

To embed JavaFX components in Swing applications, developers typically use the JFXPanel class, which serves as a bridge between Swing and JavaFX. The JFXPanel class provides a container for JavaFX content within a Swing application, allowing JavaFX components such as scenes, nodes, and controls to be seamlessly integrated into Swing-based user interfaces.

The process of embedding JavaFX components in Swing applications begins with creating an instance of the JFXPanel class and adding it to a Swing container, such as a JFrame or JPanel. This can be done programmatically in Java code using Swing APIs. For example, developers can create a new JFXPanel instance and add it to a JPanel using the add() method:

javaCopy code

```
JPanel swingPanel = new JPanel(); JFXPanel javafxPanel = new JFXPanel(); swingPanel.add(javafxPanel);
```

Once the JFXPanel is added to the Swing container, developers can initialize and configure the JavaFX content to be displayed within the panel. This typically involves creating a JavaFX scene and adding JavaFX nodes and controls to the scene. Developers can use standard JavaFX APIs to define the layout, styling, and behavior of the JavaFX content.

For example, developers can create a JavaFX scene with a button and add it to the JFXPanel:

javaCopy code

```
Platform.runLater(() -> { Button button = new Button("JavaFX Button"); Scene scene = new Scene(new Group(button), 300, 250); javafxPanel.setScene(scene); });
```

In this code snippet, the Platform.runLater() method is used to execute the JavaFX code on the JavaFX Application Thread, ensuring thread safety when interacting with JavaFX components. Inside the runLater() method, a new Button component is created, and a new Scene containing the button is created with specific dimensions. Finally, the scene is set as the content of the JFXPanel using the setScene() method.

Once the JavaFX content is configured and added to the JFXPanel, it will be displayed within the Swing container alongside other Swing components. Developers can mix and match Swing and JavaFX components within the same user interface, allowing for seamless integration of both technologies.

Deploying Swing applications with embedded JavaFX components involves packaging the application using standard Java deployment techniques. Developers can use tools such as Apache Maven or Gradle to build the application, and then package it as a standalone executable JAR file or a platform-specific installer using tools like JavaFX Packager or third-party packaging tools.

When deploying Swing applications with embedded JavaFX components, it's essential to ensure that all required JavaFX dependencies are included in the application's classpath or bundled with the application distribution. This ensures that the JavaFX runtime libraries are available at runtime when the application is executed.

In addition to embedding simple JavaFX components like buttons and labels, developers can also embed more complex JavaFX scenes and controls, such as charts, media players, and web views, into Swing applications. This allows for the creation of rich and interactive user interfaces that take advantage of the full capabilities of JavaFX.

One common use case for embedding JavaFX components in Swing applications is to modernize legacy Swing applications by adding new features and visual enhancements using JavaFX. For example, developers can replace outdated Swing components with modern JavaFX controls, add animations and transitions to improve the user experience, and integrate multimedia content such as videos and interactive charts.

Overall, embedding JavaFX components in Swing applications provides developers with a flexible and powerful approach to building modern, feature-rich user interfaces. By seamlessly integrating JavaFX and Swing technologies, developers can leverage the strengths of both platforms to create compelling user experiences for desktop and enterprise applications.

Bridging communication between JavaFX and Swing components is a crucial aspect of developing hybrid applications that leverage the strengths of both frameworks. While JavaFX and Swing offer powerful features independently, integrating them allows developers to create seamless user experiences with enhanced functionality and visual appeal.

To bridge communication between JavaFX and Swing components, developers often use techniques such as event listeners, shared data models, and message passing. These techniques enable JavaFX and Swing components to interact with each other, exchange data, and respond to user actions effectively.

One common approach to bridging communication is through event listeners. Both JavaFX and Swing components support event-driven programming models, allowing developers to register event listeners and handle user actions such as button clicks, mouse events, and keyboard input. By registering event listeners on JavaFX and Swing components, developers can synchronize the behavior of the components and ensure consistent user interactions across the application.

For example, developers can create event listeners in JavaFX to listen for user interactions with JavaFX components and trigger corresponding actions in Swing components:

javaCopy code

```
// JavaFX code Button javafxButton = new Button("JavaFX Button"); javafxButton.setOnAction(event -> { // Trigger action in Swing component swingButton.doClick(); });
```

In this code snippet, an event listener is registered on a JavaFX button to listen for button click events. When the button is clicked in the JavaFX scene, the event listener triggers an action in a Swing button by programmatically invoking its doClick() method. This allows for seamless communication between JavaFX and Swing components in response to user interactions.

Another approach to bridging communication is through shared data models. Developers can create shared data models that encapsulate application data and state, allowing JavaFX and Swing components to access and modify the same data. By synchronizing data access and updates through shared models, developers can ensure consistency and coherence between JavaFX and Swing views.

For example, developers can create a shared data model to represent application data and expose methods for accessing and updating the data:

javaCopy code

```
// Shared data model public class SharedModel { private String data; public String getData() { return data; } public void setData(String data) { this.data = data; } }
```

Both JavaFX and Swing components can then access the shared data model and interact with the data:

javaCopy code

```
// JavaFX code SharedModel sharedModel = new SharedModel(); TextField javafxTextField = new TextField();
javafxTextField.textProperty().bindBidirectional(shared
Model.dataProperty()); // Swing code SharedModel sharedModel = new SharedModel(); JTextField swingTextField = new JTextField();
swingTextField.setText(sharedModel.getData());
```

In this example, a shared data model is created to represent a text data value. In the JavaFX code, a JavaFX text field is bound bidirectionally to the data property of the shared model, allowing changes in the text field to automatically update the shared data model and vice versa. Similarly, in the Swing code, a Swing text field is initialized with the data from the shared model.

Additionally, developers can use message passing techniques to facilitate communication between JavaFX and Swing components. Message passing involves sending and receiving messages between components to convey information or trigger actions. This approach allows developers to decouple JavaFX and Swing components and promote modularity and extensibility in the application architecture.

For example, developers can implement a message passing mechanism using event bus libraries such as EventBus or JavaFX's built-in event system to publish and subscribe to events:

```java
javaCopy code
// Publish message from JavaFX component EventBus.publish(new MessageEvent("Hello from JavaFX")); // Subscribe to message in Swing component EventBus.subscribe(MessageEvent.class, event -> { System.out.println("Received message: " + event.getMessage()); });
```

In this code snippet, a message event is published from a JavaFX component using an event bus. The event is then received and processed by a Swing component subscribed to the message event. This enables communication between JavaFX and Swing components without direct coupling, promoting flexibility and maintainability in the application design.

When deploying applications that bridge communication between JavaFX and Swing components, developers should ensure compatibility with the target runtime environment and address any potential dependencies or runtime requirements. By following best practices for application deployment and distribution, developers can ensure that their hybrid JavaFX and Swing applications are deployed successfully and perform optimally across different platforms and environments.

***BOOK 4***

***EXPERT-LEVEL JAVA SWING MASTERY HARNESSING THE FULL POWER OF GUI PROGRAMMING***

***ROB BOTWRIGHT***

## Chapter 1: Advanced Custom Painting Techniques

When integrating JavaFX and Swing components within the same application, developers often encounter the need to facilitate communication between the two frameworks. This interaction allows for seamless interoperability and enables developers to leverage the strengths of both JavaFX and Swing in their applications. While JavaFX and Swing provide distinct APIs for creating graphical user interfaces, bridging communication between them can be achieved through various techniques and strategies.

One common approach to bridging communication between JavaFX and Swing components is using listeners and event handling mechanisms. Both JavaFX and Swing support event-driven programming models, where components can generate events in response to user actions or other stimuli. By registering listeners for specific events on JavaFX or Swing components, developers can capture these events and trigger corresponding actions in the other framework.

For example, in a Swing application containing a JavaFX component, developers can register a listener for a specific event, such as a button click, on the JavaFX component. When the event occurs, the listener can invoke a method in the Swing component to perform a related action. Similarly, in a JavaFX application containing Swing components, developers can use event listeners to capture events generated by Swing components and respond accordingly in JavaFX.

Another approach to bridging communication between JavaFX and Swing components is using shared data models or properties. Both frameworks support data binding and observable properties, allowing changes to one component's state to automatically propagate to other components observing the same data model. By creating shared data models or properties that are accessible to both JavaFX and Swing components, developers can ensure consistent behavior and synchronization between the two frameworks.

For example, developers can create an observable property in JavaFX representing a value that is also displayed in a Swing component. Changes to the value in either framework can be automatically reflected in the other framework through data binding mechanisms. This approach reduces the need for manual synchronization and ensures that both JavaFX and Swing components remain in sync with each other.

Additionally, developers can use direct method calls or invocations to communicate between JavaFX and Swing components. Since both JavaFX and Swing components are ultimately Java objects, developers can invoke methods on one framework's components from the other framework's code. This approach allows for direct and immediate communication between components without the need for event listeners or shared data models.

For example, developers can obtain a reference to a Swing component from JavaFX code using the

Platform.runLater() method to ensure thread safety, and then call methods on the Swing component as needed. Similarly, in Swing code, developers can obtain a reference to a JavaFX component and invoke methods on it directly.

When deploying applications that bridge communication between JavaFX and Swing components, developers should ensure that all required dependencies for both frameworks are included in the application's classpath or bundled with the application distribution. This ensures that the application can properly initialize and interact with both JavaFX and Swing components at runtime.

In summary, bridging communication between JavaFX and Swing components is essential for building hybrid applications that leverage the strengths of both frameworks. By using event listeners, shared data models, or direct method invocations, developers can enable seamless interaction between JavaFX and Swing components, resulting in more flexible and feature-rich user interfaces. Implementing custom painting with BufferedImage is a powerful technique employed in Java graphical user interface (GUI) programming to create dynamic and visually appealing graphics. BufferedImage, a subclass of Image, allows developers to create and manipulate images in memory, providing a versatile canvas for custom graphics rendering. By leveraging BufferedImage, developers can implement custom painting routines to render complex graphics, manipulate pixel data, and create sophisticated visual effects within their Java applications.

To begin implementing custom painting with BufferedImage in a Java application, developers typically start by creating an instance of BufferedImage with the desired dimensions and color model. This can be achieved using the BufferedImage constructor, specifying parameters such as width, height, and image type. For example, the following Java code snippet creates a BufferedImage with dimensions 800x600 and RGB color model:

javaCopy code

```
BufferedImage image = new BufferedImage(800, 600, BufferedImage.TYPE_INT_RGB);
```

Once the BufferedImage is created, developers can obtain a Graphics2D object associated with the image using the getGraphics() method. Graphics2D provides a comprehensive set of methods for rendering shapes, text, and images onto the BufferedImage. Developers can utilize these methods to implement custom painting routines, such as drawing lines, shapes, or text, directly onto the image.

For instance, to draw a red rectangle on the BufferedImage at coordinates (100, 100) with a width of 200 pixels and a height of 150 pixels, developers can use the following Java code:

javaCopy code

```
Graphics2D g2d = image.createGraphics(); g2d.setColor(Color.RED); g2d.fillRect(100, 100, 200, 150); g2d.dispose(); // Dispose of the Graphics2D object to release resources
```

In addition to basic shapes and colors, developers can also load existing images or create complex visual effects by manipulating pixel data directly within the BufferedImage. This level of control allows for the creation of custom image filters, transformations, and special effects.

For example, developers can iterate over each pixel in the BufferedImage, manipulate its color or intensity, and update the pixel data accordingly. This approach enables the implementation of various image processing techniques, such as grayscale conversion, edge detection, or blur effects.

javaCopy code

```
// Iterate over each pixel in the BufferedImage for (int y = 0; y < image.getHeight(); y++) { for (int x = 0; x < image.getWidth(); x++) { // Get the color of the pixel at coordinates (x, y) int rgb = image.getRGB(x, y); // Extract individual color components (red, green, blue) from the pixel int red = (rgb >> 16) & 0xFF; int green = (rgb >> 8) & 0xFF; int blue = rgb & 0xFF; // Apply grayscale conversion by averaging color components int gray = (red + green + blue) / 3; // Set the new color for the pixel int newRGB = (gray << 16) | (gray << 8) | gray; image.setRGB(x, y, newRGB); } }
```

Once the custom painting operations are performed on the BufferedImage, developers can render the image onto a Swing component, such as a JPanel, to display it within the user interface. This is typically accomplished by overriding the paintComponent() method of the

Swing component and using the Graphics object provided to draw the BufferedImage.

javaCopy code

```
@Override protected void paintComponent(Graphics g) { super.paintComponent(g); // Draw the BufferedImage onto the JPanel g.drawImage(image, 0, 0, null); }
```

In addition to displaying the BufferedImage within a Swing component, developers can also save the image to disk or perform further processing, such as image analysis or recognition. This versatility makes BufferedImage a valuable tool for a wide range of applications, including image editing software, data visualization tools, and computer-aided design (CAD) applications.

Overall, implementing custom painting with BufferedImage in Java provides developers with a flexible and powerful means of creating dynamic and visually compelling graphics within their applications. By leveraging BufferedImage's capabilities for rendering shapes, manipulating pixel data, and applying image effects, developers can create sophisticated visualizations and enhance the user experience of their Java applications.

## Chapter 2: Creating Rich User Interfaces with JLayeredPane

Layering components for depth and interaction is a fundamental aspect of creating rich and interactive user interfaces in Java Swing applications. By strategically arranging components on different layers, developers can achieve depth perception, enhance visual hierarchy, and facilitate user interaction with various elements within the interface. This technique involves leveraging Swing's layered pane container, which allows components to be stacked on top of each other, enabling flexible and dynamic layout arrangements.

To begin layering components, developers typically utilize Swing's JLayeredPane class, which serves as a container for managing the stacking order of components. The JLayeredPane provides several layers, each represented by an integer value, where components with higher layer values are rendered above those with lower layer values. By adding components to specific layers within the JLayeredPane, developers can control their visibility and interaction priority.

One common use case of layering components is creating overlays or pop-up dialogs that appear above the main content of the application. For example, developers can use a higher layer to display modal dialogs, tooltips, or context menus, ensuring that these components remain visible and interactable regardless of the underlying content. This approach enhances user experience by providing contextual information or options without obstructing the main interface.

javaCopy code

```
JLayeredPane layeredPane = new JLayeredPane(); layeredPane.setPreferredSize( new Dimension(800, 600)); JPanel mainPanel = new JPanel(); // Add main content components to the default layer (0) layeredPane.add(mainPanel, JLayeredPane.DEFAULT_LAYER); JDialog dialog = new JDialog(); // Add modal dialog to a higher layer (100) layeredPane.add(dialog.getContentPane(), JLayeredPane.MODAL_LAYER); // Display the layered pane within a JFrame or other top-level container
```

Another use case for layering components is creating immersive user interfaces with depth perception. By placing components on different layers and applying visual effects such as shadows, gradients, or transparency, developers can simulate a three-dimensional environment and create a sense of depth within the interface. This technique is particularly effective for designing interactive applications, such as games or multimedia presentations, where visual aesthetics play a crucial role in user engagement.

javaCopy code

```
// Example of creating a custom component with shadow effect public class ShadowPanel extends JPanel { @Override protected void paintComponent(Graphics g) {
```

super.paintComponent(g); Graphics2D g2d = (Graphics2D) g; g2d.setColor(Color.LIGHT_GRAY); g2d.setComposite(AlphaComposite.getInstance(AlphaComposite.SRC_OVER, 0.5f)); g2d.fillRect(5, 5, getWidth() - 10, getHeight() - 10); } }

In addition to visual depth, layering components enables developers to implement interactive features such as drag-and-drop functionality or custom event handling. By placing draggable components on a dedicated layer and implementing mouse listeners to detect drag events, developers can create intuitive user interfaces where users can interact with objects within the interface seamlessly.

javaCopy code

```java
// Example of implementing drag-and-drop functionality with layered components JLabel draggableLabel = new JLabel("Drag me!"); draggableLabel.addMouseListener(new MouseAdapter() { public void mousePressed(MouseEvent e) { layeredPane.setLayer(draggableLabel, JLayeredPane.DRAG_LAYER); draggableLabel.setLocation(e.getX(), e.getY()); layeredPane.add(draggableLabel); } public void mouseReleased(MouseEvent e) { layeredPane.setLayer(draggableLabel, JLayeredPane.DEFAULT_LAYER); } });
```

Furthermore, layering components allows developers to manage complex layouts and organize the interface into logical layers based on functionality or content type. For example, developers can create separate layers for user interface elements, background graphics, interactive widgets, or multimedia content, enabling finer control over the visual presentation and interaction behavior of each component.

Overall, layering components for depth and interaction is a versatile technique that empowers developers to create dynamic, immersive, and interactive user interfaces in Java Swing applications. By leveraging Swing's JLayeredPane container and strategically arranging components on different layers, developers can enhance the visual aesthetics, usability, and functionality of their applications, ultimately delivering a more engaging and intuitive user experience.

Creating dynamic overlay components is a crucial technique in modern GUI development, allowing developers to display temporary or context-sensitive information on top of existing interface elements. These overlays can provide additional functionality, contextual help, or visual feedback to users, enhancing the overall user experience. In Java Swing applications, achieving dynamic overlays involves dynamically adding and removing components to the UI hierarchy based on user interactions or application state changes.

One common scenario where dynamic overlays are used is displaying tooltips or pop-up messages when users hover over specific UI elements. To implement this functionality in Swing, developers can leverage mouse listeners to detect mouse movements and dynamically add tooltip components to the UI when needed. By attaching a mouse listener to relevant UI components and listening for mouse-enter and mouse-exit events, developers can show and hide tooltip overlays accordingly.

javaCopy code

```
// Example of adding tooltip overlays with mouse listeners JButton button = new JButton("Hover Me"); button.addMouseListener(new MouseAdapter() { public void mouseEntered(MouseEvent e) { showTooltip(e.getX(), e.getY(), "Tooltip Message"); } public void mouseExited(MouseEvent e) { hideTooltip(); } }); private void showTooltip(int x, int y, String message) { // Create and display tooltip component at the specified location } private void hideTooltip() { // Hide tooltip component }
```

Another use case for dynamic overlays is implementing context menus or pop-up dialogs that appear when users right-click on specific UI elements. To achieve this in Swing, developers can listen for mouse right-click events and display custom pop-up menus or dialogs at the cursor's position. By associating a mouse listener with relevant UI components and handling mouse right-click events, developers can trigger the display of context-sensitive overlays.

javaCopy code

```
// Example of displaying context menu overlay with mouse listener JPanel panel = new JPanel(); panel.addMouseListener(new MouseAdapter() {
```

public void mouseClicked(MouseEvent e) { if (SwingUtilities.isRightMouseButton(e)) { showContextMenu(e.getX(), e.getY()); } } }); private void showContextMenu(int x, int y) { // Create and display context menu at the specified location }

Dynamic overlays are also useful for presenting modal dialogs or notifications that require user interaction or attention. For instance, developers can create custom dialog components or notification panels and dynamically add them to the UI hierarchy when certain application events occur. By managing the visibility and content of these overlay components programmatically, developers can provide timely and context-aware feedback to users.

javaCopy code

```
// Example of displaying modal dialog overlay programmatically public void showMessageDialog(String message) { JDialog dialog = new JDialog(); JLabel label = new JLabel(message); dialog.add(label); dialog.pack(); dialog.setModal(true); dialog.setLocationRelativeTo(null); dialog.setVisible(true); }
```

Furthermore, dynamic overlays can be used to highlight or annotate specific areas of the interface, such as indicating validation errors in form fields or drawing attention to important UI elements. By dynamically adding visual overlays, such as colored borders or animated effects, developers can draw users' attention to relevant parts of the interface and provide guidance or feedback as needed.

In summary, creating dynamic overlay components is a versatile technique that enables developers to enhance the functionality, usability, and visual appeal of Java Swing applications. By dynamically adding and removing components to the UI hierarchy based on user interactions or application state changes, developers can provide context-sensitive information, facilitate user interaction, and improve the overall user experience. Whether it's displaying tooltips, context menus, modal dialogs, or visual highlights, dynamic overlays play a crucial role in creating intuitive and engaging GUIs.

## Chapter 3: Mastering the SwingWorker API for Asynchronous Tasks

SwingWorker is a powerful utility class in the Java Swing framework that facilitates background processing of tasks without freezing the user interface. In modern GUI applications, it's essential to perform time-consuming operations, such as data fetching, computation, or file I/O, in a separate thread to maintain UI responsiveness. SwingWorker simplifies this process by providing a convenient way to execute tasks asynchronously and update Swing components safely from the background thread.

One common scenario where SwingWorker is invaluable is when performing network operations or accessing external resources that may cause the UI to become unresponsive if executed on the Event Dispatch Thread (EDT). For instance, fetching data from a remote server or downloading files from the internet can lead to delays in UI responsiveness if executed synchronously. By offloading such tasks to a SwingWorker thread, developers can prevent the UI from freezing and provide a smoother user experience.

javaCopy code

```
// Example of using SwingWorker for background network operation public class NetworkTask extends SwingWorker<Void, Void> { protected Void doInBackground() { // Perform network operation in background thread return null; } protected void
```

done() { // Update UI or perform post-processing when task completes } } // Usage: NetworkTask task = new NetworkTask(); task.execute();

SwingWorker operates by executing the time-consuming task in a background thread while allowing developers to update Swing components safely from within designated callback methods. The **doInBackground()** method is overridden to perform the actual task in the background thread, while the **done()** method is invoked when the task completes, allowing developers to update the UI or perform any necessary post-processing.

Another use case for SwingWorker is performing CPU-intensive computations or data processing tasks that could potentially block the EDT if executed synchronously. By delegating such tasks to a background thread, developers can ensure that the UI remains responsive and continues to handle user interactions smoothly.

javaCopy code

// Example of using SwingWorker for CPU-intensive computation public class ComputationTask extends SwingWorker<Integer, Void> { protected Integer doInBackground() { // Perform CPU-intensive computation in background thread return result; } protected void done() { try { int result = get(); // Update UI with computation result } catch (InterruptedException | ExecutionException ex) { //

Handle exception } } } // Usage: ComputationTask task = new ComputationTask(); task.execute();

In addition to executing background tasks, SwingWorker also supports progress reporting and cancellation. Developers can update the progress of a task and listen for progress changes using the **publish()** and **process()** methods. Furthermore, tasks can be cancelled using the **cancel()** method, allowing users to interrupt long-running operations if needed.

javaCopy code

// Example of reporting progress in SwingWorker public class ProgressTask extends SwingWorker<Void, Integer> { protected Void doInBackground() { for (int i = 0; i < 100; i++) { // Perform task iteration publish(i); // Report progress } return null; } protected void process(List<Integer> chunks) { int progress = chunks.get(chunks.size() - 1); // Update progress bar or UI with current progress } } // Usage: ProgressTask task = new ProgressTask(); task.execute();

Overall, SwingWorker is a versatile tool for handling background processing in Java Swing applications. By executing time-consuming tasks in separate threads and providing mechanisms for progress reporting and cancellation, SwingWorker enables developers to create responsive and interactive GUIs that can handle complex operations without sacrificing user experience.

Handling SwingWorker's progress and completion is crucial for providing a smooth and responsive user experience in Java Swing applications. SwingWorker is a powerful tool for executing long-running tasks in the background while keeping the UI thread free to respond to user interactions. However, to effectively utilize SwingWorker, developers need to implement mechanisms to track the progress of tasks and handle their completion.

One common approach to handling progress in SwingWorker is to report intermediate results or progress updates to the UI thread. This can be achieved using the **publish()** and **process()** methods provided by SwingWorker. Inside the **doInBackground()** method, developers can periodically publish progress updates using the **publish()** method, passing the intermediate results as parameters. The **process()** method, which runs on the Event Dispatch Thread (EDT), then receives these updates and can update the UI accordingly.

javaCopy code

```
// Example of reporting progress in SwingWorker public class ProgressTask extends SwingWorker<Void, Integer> { protected Void doInBackground() { for (int i = 0; i < 100; i++) { // Perform task iteration publish(i); // Report progress } return null; } protected void process(List<Integer> chunks) { int progress = chunks.get(chunks.size() - 1); // Update progress bar or UI with current progress } } // Usage: ProgressTask task = new ProgressTask(); task.execute();
```

In this example, the **ProgressTask** class extends SwingWorker and overrides the **doInBackground()** method to perform a long-running task. Inside the loop, the task publishes progress updates using the **publish()** method. The **process()** method receives these updates on the EDT and updates the UI accordingly. This allows users to see the progress of the task in real-time, providing feedback and enhancing the user experience.

Besides reporting progress, it's also essential to handle the completion of SwingWorker tasks appropriately. The **done()** method, provided by SwingWorker, is invoked when the background task completes, either successfully or due to an error. Developers can override this method to perform any necessary cleanup or post-processing tasks, such as updating the UI with the final result or handling exceptions gracefully.

javaCopy code

```
// Example of handling task completion in SwingWorker public class CompletionTask extends SwingWorker<Void, Void> { protected Void doInBackground() { // Perform background task return null; } protected void done() { try { get(); // Retrieve result (if any) // Task completed successfully // Update UI or perform post-processing } catch (InterruptedException | ExecutionException ex) { // Handle exception } } } // Usage: CompletionTask task = new CompletionTask(); task.execute();
```

In this example, the **CompletionTask** class extends SwingWorker and overrides the **doInBackground()** method to perform a background task. Inside the **done()** method, the task checks for any exceptions that may have occurred during execution and handles them appropriately. If the task completes successfully, developers can update the UI or perform any necessary post-processing.

Overall, handling SwingWorker's progress and completion is essential for creating responsive and user-friendly Swing applications. By reporting progress updates to the UI thread and handling task completion gracefully, developers can ensure that users have a smooth and enjoyable experience while interacting with their applications.

## Chapter 4: Advanced Event Dispatching and Event Queues

Understanding Event Dispatch Thread (EDT) optimization is crucial for developing efficient and responsive Java Swing applications. The EDT is a dedicated thread responsible for handling user interface events, such as user input, component repaint requests, and event listeners' callbacks. In Swing, all UI-related activities should occur on the EDT to ensure thread safety and prevent potential concurrency issues. However, performing lengthy or blocking tasks on the EDT can lead to unresponsive user interfaces and poor user experience.

To optimize EDT performance, developers need to follow best practices and utilize techniques such as offloading time-consuming tasks to background threads, minimizing EDT blocking operations, and prioritizing UI responsiveness. One common approach is to use SwingWorker or other concurrency utilities provided by Java to execute lengthy tasks asynchronously on background threads while keeping the EDT free to process user input and update the UI.

javaCopy code

```
// Example of using SwingWorker to offload tasks from EDT SwingWorker<Void, Void> worker = new SwingWorker<Void, Void>() { @Override protected Void doInBackground() throws Exception { // Perform lengthy task in background thread return null; }
```

```
@Override protected void done() { // Update UI or perform post-processing on EDT } }; worker.execute(); // Start the background task
```

By offloading tasks from the EDT, developers can prevent UI freezes and maintain a responsive user interface. Additionally, it's essential to minimize EDT blocking operations, such as long-running computations, I/O operations, or database queries. Performing these operations on the EDT can cause the UI to become unresponsive until the task completes, leading to a poor user experience. Instead, developers should perform such operations on background threads and update the UI asynchronously when the task finishes.

Another aspect of EDT optimization is prioritizing UI responsiveness by breaking down complex tasks into smaller, incremental updates and interleaving them with UI refreshes. For example, when processing a large dataset or performing complex calculations, developers can update the UI periodically with partial results or progress indicators to maintain responsiveness and keep users informed about the ongoing task's status.

Furthermore, developers should be mindful of excessive event generation and event listeners' overhead, which can impact EDT performance, especially in large Swing applications with numerous components and event listeners. Minimizing unnecessary event propagation and optimizing event handling logic can help reduce EDT workload and improve overall application responsiveness.

In addition to these techniques, understanding Swing's painting and rendering mechanism is essential for EDT optimization. Swing employs a lightweight rendering model where components are responsible for painting themselves rather than relying on the operating system's native windowing system. By optimizing custom painting code and minimizing unnecessary repaint requests, developers can reduce EDT workload and enhance application performance.

Overall, understanding EDT optimization is essential for building responsive and efficient Java Swing applications. By following best practices, offloading lengthy tasks from the EDT, minimizing blocking operations, prioritizing UI responsiveness, and optimizing event handling and painting logic, developers can create smooth and enjoyable user experiences in their Swing applications.

Managing high-volume event processing with event queues is a critical aspect of developing responsive and scalable software applications. In modern software systems, especially those with graphical user interfaces (GUIs), the volume of events generated by user interactions, external systems, or internal processes can be substantial. Effectively handling these events to ensure timely processing and maintain application responsiveness is essential for delivering a seamless user experience.

Event queues serve as a mechanism for organizing and prioritizing incoming events for processing. They provide a structured way to manage event flow,

allowing developers to control how events are processed and ensure that critical events receive prompt attention while preventing event overload and potential application instability.
One common use case for event queues is in GUI applications, where user interactions generate a variety of events, such as mouse clicks, keyboard inputs, and window resize events. These events must be processed efficiently to update the UI and respond to user actions in real-time. By utilizing event queues, developers can manage the flow of these events, prioritize them based on their importance or time sensitivity, and ensure that the UI remains responsive even under heavy load.
In Java Swing applications, the Event Dispatch Thread (EDT) serves as the event queue for processing UI-related events. All GUI events, such as user input and component repaint requests, are dispatched and processed on the EDT to maintain thread safety and prevent UI concurrency issues. However, processing lengthy or blocking tasks on the EDT can lead to UI freezes and degrade application performance.
To manage high-volume event processing in Swing applications, developers can utilize additional event queues for handling non-UI-related events or offloading time-consuming tasks from the EDT. This approach ensures that the EDT remains free to process UI events, while background threads or worker threads handle other types of events asynchronously.
One way to implement event queues in Java Swing is by using the java.util.concurrent package, which provides various concurrency utilities, including BlockingQueue

implementations for managing event queues. Developers can create custom event queues using classes such as LinkedBlockingQueue or ArrayBlockingQueue to store incoming events and process them asynchronously in worker threads.

javaCopy code

```java
// Example of using a BlockingQueue for event processing BlockingQueue<Event> eventQueue = new LinkedBlockingQueue<>(); // Producer thread adds events to the queue Thread producerThread = new Thread(() -> { while (true) { Event event = getNextEvent(); eventQueue.offer(event); // Add event to the queue } }); producerThread.start(); // Consumer thread processes events from the queue Thread consumerThread = new Thread(() -> { while (true) { try { Event event = eventQueue.take(); // Retrieve and remove event from the queue processEvent(event); // Process the event } catch (InterruptedException e) { Thread.currentThread().interrupt(); // Restore interrupted status } } }); consumerThread.start();
```

By decoupling event generation from event processing and using event queues to buffer and prioritize incoming events, developers can effectively manage high-volume event processing in Swing applications while maintaining responsiveness and scalability. Additionally, event queues enable developers to implement advanced event handling strategies, such as event batching, throttling, and load balancing, to optimize application performance and resource utilization.

In summary, managing high-volume event processing with event queues is essential for developing responsive and scalable software applications, particularly in GUI applications like Java Swing. By utilizing event queues to buffer and prioritize incoming events, developers can ensure timely event processing, maintain application responsiveness, and deliver a seamless user experience even under heavy load.

## Chapter 5: Advanced Animation Techniques with Timing Framework

Smooth animation transitions play a crucial role in enhancing the visual appeal and user experience of software applications. Whether in games, multimedia presentations, or graphical user interfaces (GUIs), animations that transition seamlessly between different states or properties can significantly contribute to the overall polished look and feel of an application. One powerful tool for achieving smooth animation transitions in Java applications is the Timing Framework.
The Timing Framework is an open-source library developed by the Java Desktop Team at Sun Microsystems (now part of Oracle). It provides a flexible and easy-to-use framework for creating and controlling animations in Java applications. With the Timing Framework, developers can define animations that smoothly transition between different states or properties over a specified duration, allowing for visually appealing effects such as fading, scaling, rotating, and translating graphical elements.
One of the key features of the Timing Framework is its support for interpolation, which enables animations to smoothly transition between start and end values over time. Interpolation calculates intermediate values based on predefined easing functions, such as linear, ease-in, ease-out, and ease-in-out, to achieve gradual changes in animation properties. This allows developers to create

animations that accelerate or decelerate smoothly, mimicking natural motion and enhancing the overall user experience.

To utilize the Timing Framework in Java applications, developers need to include the timingframework.jar file in their project's classpath. This can be done using a build tool like Apache Maven or by manually adding the JAR file to the project's dependencies.

bashCopy code

```
# Example Maven dependency configuration for Timing
Framework <dependency>
<groupId>org.jdesktop</groupId>
<artifactId>timingframework</artifactId>
<version>1.0</version> </dependency>
```

Once the Timing Framework is included in the project, developers can start creating animations using its API. The framework provides classes such as Animator, PropertySetter, and TimingTarget to define and control animations. Here's a basic example of how to create a simple fade-in animation using the Timing Framework:

javaCopy code

```
import org.jdesktop.core.animation.timing.Animator;
import
org.jdesktop.core.animation.timing.TimingSource;
import
org.jdesktop.core.animation.timing.TimingTargetAdapt
er; import javax.swing.*; import java.awt.*; public
class FadeInAnimationExample { public static void
main(String[] args) {
```

SwingUtilities.invokeLater(FadeInAnimationExample::createAndShowGUI); } private static void createAndShowGUI() { JFrame frame = new JFrame("Fade-In Animation Example"); frame.setDefaultCloseOperation(JFrame.EXIT_ON_CLOSE); frame.setSize(400, 300); frame.setLocationRelativeTo(null); JLabel label = new JLabel("Hello, Timing Framework!"); label.setFont(new Font("Arial", Font.PLAIN, 24)); label.setHorizontalAlignment(SwingConstants.CENTER); frame.add(label); // Create an animator for fading in the label Animator animator = new Animator.Builder().setDuration(1000) // 1 second duration .setEndFraction(1.0f) // End opacity (fully opaque) .setInterpolator(new Animator.DefaultInterpolator(Interpolator.EASE_IN)) // Ease-in interpolation .addTarget(new TimingTargetAdapter() { @Override public void timingEvent(float fraction) { label.setOpaque(true); label.setForeground(new Color(0, 0, 0, (int) (255 * fraction))); // Update label opacity } }) .build(); frame.setVisible(true); animator.start(); // Start the animation } }

In this example, we create a JFrame with a JLabel containing some text. We then define an Animator object that fades in the label over a duration of 1 second using an ease-in interpolation. The TimingTargetAdapter class is used to define the

behavior of the animation, updating the label's opacity as the animation progresses.
By incorporating the Timing Framework into Java applications, developers can easily create smooth animation transitions that enhance the visual appeal and user experience of their software. Whether used in games, multimedia applications, or GUIs, the Timing Framework provides a powerful and flexible solution for creating dynamic and engaging animations.

Creating complex animation sequences is a fundamental aspect of developing dynamic and engaging user interfaces and multimedia applications. These sequences involve orchestrating multiple animations to achieve sophisticated effects, such as transitions between different states, interactive behaviors, and storytelling elements. In Java applications, developers can leverage various techniques and libraries to create such complex animation sequences, including combining multiple timing mechanisms, controlling animation flow, and synchronizing animations with user interactions.
One approach to creating complex animation sequences in Java applications is to utilize the Timing Framework library, which provides a powerful API for defining and controlling animations. With the Timing Framework, developers can orchestrate multiple animations in sequence or parallel, allowing for the creation of intricate and dynamic effects. By combining different easing functions, interpolation techniques, and timing parameters, developers can achieve smooth transitions

between different animation states and create visually appealing sequences.

To illustrate the process of creating complex animation sequences with the Timing Framework, let's consider an example scenario where we want to animate a series of graphical elements to simulate a bouncing ball effect. We'll create a Java Swing application that displays a ball moving vertically within a window, bouncing off the top and bottom edges. We'll use the Timing Framework to control the ball's motion and simulate realistic physics behavior.

First, we need to include the Timing Framework library in our project's dependencies. If we're using Maven, we can add the following dependency to our project's pom.xml file:

xmlCopy code

```
<dependency>        <groupId>org.jdesktop</groupId>
<artifactId>timingframework</artifactId>
<version>1.0</version> </dependency>
```

Next, we'll create a Ball class that represents the graphical ball element. The Ball class will have properties such as position, velocity, and acceleration, and methods to update its state based on the current animation time. We'll also define a BallAnimator class that extends TimingTargetAdapter and controls the animation of the ball.

javaCopy code

```
import    org.jdesktop.core.animation.timing.Animator;
import
org.jdesktop.core.animation.timing.TimingTargetAdapt
```

er; import org.jdesktop.swing.animation.timing.sources.SwingTimerTimingSource; import javax.swing.*; import java.awt.*; public class BallAnimationExample { public static void main(String[] args) { SwingUtilities.invokeLater(BallAnimationExample::createAndShowGUI); } private static void createAndShowGUI() { JFrame frame = new JFrame("Ball Animation Example"); frame.setDefaultCloseOperation(JFrame.EXIT_ON_CLOSE); frame.setSize(400, 300); frame.setLocationRelativeTo(null); BallPanel ballPanel = new BallPanel(); frame.add(ballPanel); frame.setVisible(true); BallAnimator ballAnimator = new BallAnimator(ballPanel); ballAnimator.start(); } } class BallPanel extends JPanel { private static final int BALL_SIZE = 20; private int ballY = 0; @Override protected void paintComponent(Graphics g) { super.paintComponent(g); g.setColor(Color.RED); g.fillOval(180, ballY, BALL_SIZE, BALL_SIZE); } public void setBallY(int ballY) { this.ballY = ballY; repaint(); } } class BallAnimator extends TimingTargetAdapter { private static final int ANIMATION_DURATION = 2000; // 2 seconds private BallPanel ballPanel; private Animator animator; public BallAnimator(BallPanel ballPanel) { this.ballPanel = ballPanel; this.animator = new Animator.Builder(new

SwingTimerTimingSource (), this) .setDuration(ANIMATION_DURATION) .build(); } public void start() { animator.start(); } @Override public void timingEvent(float fraction) { // Update ball position based on animation fraction int maxHeight = ballPanel.getHeight() - 20; int newY = (int) (fraction * maxHeight); ballPanel.setBallY(newY); } }

In this example, we create a JFrame with a BallPanel, which is a custom JPanel subclass responsible for drawing the ball. We define a BallAnimator class that controls the animation of the ball using the Timing Framework. The BallAnimator class extends TimingTargetAdapter and implements the timingEvent method to update the ball's position based on the animation fraction.

When the application starts, the ball animates smoothly from the top to the bottom of the window over a 2-second duration. By adjusting the timing parameters and interpolation functions, developers can customize the animation sequence to achieve desired effects.

In summary, creating complex animation sequences in Java applications involves orchestrating multiple animations to achieve sophisticated visual effects. By leveraging libraries like the Timing Framework and techniques such as combining timing mechanisms, controlling animation flow, and synchronizing animations with user interactions, developers can create dynamic and engaging user interfaces and multimedia applications.

## Chapter 6: High-Performance Rendering with Buffered Images

BufferedImage is a versatile and powerful class in Java's ImageIO package that allows developers to perform efficient image manipulation tasks. It provides a convenient way to work with images in various formats and perform operations such as loading, processing, and saving images. Utilizing BufferedImage for image manipulation tasks is essential for many Java applications, including graphic editors, image processing tools, and multimedia applications.

One common task where BufferedImage is invaluable is image loading and rendering in Java applications. To load an image using BufferedImage, developers can use the **ImageIO.read(File)** method, passing the image file as a parameter. For example, to load an image named "image.jpg" from the filesystem, the following command can be used:

javaCopy code

```
File imageFile = new File("image.jpg");
BufferedImage image = ImageIO.read(imageFile);
```

This command loads the image file into a BufferedImage object, allowing developers to access and manipulate its pixels easily. Once loaded, developers can perform various operations on the image, such as resizing, cropping, rotating, and applying filters.

Resizing an image is a common operation performed using BufferedImage. Developers can resize an image to a specific width and height using the **Graphics2D.drawImage()** method. For example, to resize an image to 300x200 pixels, the following code snippet can be used:

javaCopy code

```
int newWidth = 300; int newHeight = 200; BufferedImage resizedImage = new BufferedImage(newWidth, newHeight, BufferedImage.TYPE_INT_RGB); Graphics2D g2d = resizedImage.createGraphics();
g2d.drawImage(originalImage, 0, 0, newWidth, newHeight, null); g2d.dispose();
```

This code creates a new BufferedImage with the specified width and height and draws the original image onto it using the **drawImage()** method.

Another common task is image cropping, where a portion of the image is extracted. BufferedImage provides methods to create a subimage from an existing image. For example, to crop a 100x100 pixel region starting at coordinates (50, 50) from the original image, the following code can be used:

javaCopy code

```
int x = 50; int y = 50; int width = 100; int height = 100; BufferedImage croppedImage = originalImage.getSubimage(x, y, width, height);
```

This code extracts a subimage from the original image starting at coordinates (50, 50) with a width and height of 100 pixels each.

In addition to basic image manipulation operations, BufferedImage also provides support for more advanced image processing tasks, such as applying image filters and transformations. Image filters can be used to enhance or modify the appearance of images, such as blurring, sharpening, or adjusting color levels.

For example, to apply a blur filter to an image, developers can use the **ConvolveOp** class in combination with a predefined kernel matrix. The following code snippet demonstrates how to apply a blur filter to an image:

javaCopy code

```
float[] blurMatrix = { 0.111f, 0.111f, 0.111f, 0.111f, 0.111f, 0.111f, 0.111f, 0.111f, 0.111f }; BufferedImageOp blurFilter = new ConvolveOp(new Kernel(3, 3, blurMatrix)); BufferedImage blurredImage = blurFilter.filter(originalImage, null);
```

This code creates a blur filter using a 3x3 matrix with equal weights for each pixel and applies it to the original image using the **filter()** method.

Furthermore, BufferedImage can be used for image analysis tasks, such as extracting image metadata, detecting features, and performing image recognition. By accessing the individual pixels of a BufferedImage, developers can analyze and manipulate the image data to extract useful information or perform advanced image processing algorithms.

In summary, BufferedImage is a versatile class in Java for efficient image manipulation tasks. By utilizing BufferedImage, developers can perform various operations on images, such as loading, resizing, cropping, applying filters, and performing advanced image processing tasks. Whether building graphic editors, image processing tools, or multimedia applications, BufferedImage provides the necessary tools to work with images effectively in Java applications.

Caching and reusing buffered images is a crucial technique for optimizing performance in Java applications, especially those involving frequent image loading and rendering tasks. By caching buffered images, developers can reduce the overhead associated with loading and processing images, leading to improved application responsiveness and reduced memory usage.

The process of caching buffered images involves storing previously loaded images in memory so that they can be quickly retrieved and reused when needed. This is particularly beneficial in scenarios where the same image is used multiple times within an application or across different application sessions.

One common approach to caching buffered images is to use a cache data structure, such as a HashMap or ConcurrentHashMap, to store the images along with their corresponding keys. When an image is needed, the application checks if it exists in the cache. If the image is found, it is retrieved from the cache; otherwise, it is loaded from the source and added to the cache for future use.

javaCopy code

```
// Initialize a cache to store buffered images
Map<String, BufferedImage> imageCache = new
```

ConcurrentHashMap<>(); // Method to load and cache an image public BufferedImage loadImage(String imagePath) { BufferedImage image = imageCache.get(imagePath); if (image == null) { // Image not found in cache, load it from the source image = loadAndProcessImage(imagePath); // Cache the image imageCache.put(imagePath, image); } return image; }

In this example, the **loadImage()** method checks if the requested image exists in the cache. If it does, the cached image is returned. Otherwise, the image is loaded from the source using a helper method (**loadAndProcessImage()**) and then added to the cache.

By caching buffered images in this manner, applications can avoid the overhead of repeatedly loading and processing the same images, resulting in faster image rendering and improved overall performance.

Additionally, developers can implement cache eviction strategies to manage the size of the image cache and prevent excessive memory consumption. One common approach is to use a least recently used (LRU) eviction policy, where the least recently accessed images are removed from the cache when it reaches a certain size limit.

javaCopy code

// Cache size limit private static final int CACHE_SIZE_LIMIT = 100; // Method to load and cache an image with LRU eviction public BufferedImage loadImageWithLRUEviction(String imagePath) { BufferedImage image = imageCache.get(imagePath); if (image == null) { // Image not found in cache, load it from the source image = loadAndProcessImage(imagePath); // Cache the image imageCache.put(imagePath, image); // Check if cache size exceeds the limit, evict least recently used image if necessary if (imageCache.size() > CACHE_SIZE_LIMIT) { evictLRUImage(); } } return image; } // Method to evict least recently used image from the cache private void evictLRUImage() { String leastRecentlyUsedKey = imageCache.keySet().iterator().next(); imageCache.remove(leastRecentlyUsedKey); }

In this example, the **loadImageWithLRUEviction()** method implements an LRU eviction policy by removing the least recently accessed image from the cache when it exceeds the specified size limit. This helps ensure that the cache remains within a manageable size while still providing efficient image retrieval.

In summary, caching and reusing buffered images is an effective technique for optimizing performance in Java applications. By storing frequently used images in memory and implementing cache eviction strategies, developers can reduce the overhead of image loading and processing, resulting in improved application responsiveness and resource utilization.

## Chapter 7: Implementing Real-Time Data Visualization

Displaying real-time data streams with charts is a fundamental aspect of many modern applications, particularly those dealing with monitoring, analytics, and IoT (Internet of Things) data visualization. Charts provide an intuitive way to visualize complex data sets, allowing users to quickly identify patterns, trends, and anomalies in the data. Whether it's monitoring stock prices, tracking sensor readings, or analyzing website traffic in real-time, displaying data with charts enhances understanding and decision-making.

To implement real-time data visualization with charts, developers typically leverage libraries or frameworks that provide charting capabilities. One popular choice for Java applications is JFreeChart, a powerful open-source library for creating professional-quality charts. Another option is JavaFX, which offers built-in support for creating interactive charts through its charting API.

Before diving into the implementation details, it's essential to understand the types of charts that are suitable for displaying real-time data streams. Line charts, area charts, and scatter plots are commonly used for visualizing time-series data, such as stock prices or sensor readings over time. Bar charts and pie charts are more suitable for categorical data, such as market share or distribution of website traffic by source.

Once the appropriate chart type is chosen based on the nature of the data, developers can start implementing the real-time data visualization functionality. In JavaFX, this typically involves creating a chart component, defining axes, and updating the chart with new data points as they arrive. Here's a simplified example of how to display real-time data streams with a line chart using JavaFX:

javaCopy code

```
import javafx.application.Application; import javafx.scene.Scene; import javafx.scene.chart.LineChart; import javafx.scene.chart.NumberAxis; import javafx.scene.chart.XYChart; import javafx.stage.Stage; public class RealTimeChartApp extends Application { private XYChart.Series<Number, Number> series = new XYChart.Series<>(); @Override public void start(Stage primaryStage) { // Create a line chart NumberAxis xAxis = new NumberAxis(); NumberAxis yAxis = new NumberAxis(); LineChart<Number, Number> lineChart = new LineChart<>(xAxis, yAxis); lineChart.setTitle("Real-Time Data Stream"); lineChart.getData().add(series); // Create a scene and add the chart Scene scene = new Scene(lineChart, 800, 600); primaryStage.setScene(scene); primaryStage.show(); // Simulate real-time data updates simulateRealTimeData(); } private void simulateRealTimeData() { // Simulate data updates
```

every second new Thread(() -> { try { for (int i = 0; i < 100; i++) { Thread.sleep(1000); double x = i; double y = Math.random() * 100; // Random data value updateChartData(x, y); } } catch (InterruptedException e) { e.printStackTrace(); } }).start(); } private void updateChartData(double x, double y) { // Add new data point to the series series.getData().add(new XYChart.Data<>(x, y)); // Remove oldest data point if series exceeds a certain size if (series.getData().size() > 50) { series.getData().remove(0); } } public static void main(String[] args) { launch(args); } }

In this example, a JavaFX application is created with a line chart to display real-time data. The **simulateRealTimeData()** method generates random data points every second to simulate real-time data updates. The **updateChartData()** method adds new data points to the chart series and removes the oldest data point if the series exceeds a certain size, ensuring that the chart remains responsive and does not consume excessive memory.

While JavaFX provides a built-in charting API, developers can also integrate third-party charting libraries like JFreeChart into their Swing applications to achieve similar real-time data visualization capabilities. JFreeChart offers support for various chart types, including line charts, bar charts, pie charts, and more, making it a versatile choice for displaying real-time data streams in Swing applications.

Overall, displaying real-time data streams with charts is a valuable technique for enhancing the usability and effectiveness of Java applications across various domains. Whether it's monitoring system metrics, analyzing financial data, or visualizing sensor readings, real-time data visualization empowers users to make informed decisions and respond promptly to changing conditions. By leveraging the capabilities of charting libraries and frameworks, developers can create compelling and interactive data visualizations that drive insights and drive business value.

Customizing data visualization for dynamic updates is a crucial aspect of modern applications, particularly those dealing with real-time data streams or frequently changing datasets. The ability to update visualizations dynamically enables users to interact with and analyze data in real-time, leading to better insights and decision-making. Whether it's monitoring stock prices, tracking sensor readings, or analyzing social media trends, customizing data visualizations for dynamic updates enhances the user experience and improves the utility of the application.

To achieve dynamic updates in data visualization, developers need to consider several factors, including the choice of visualization library or framework, the type of data being visualized, and the frequency of updates. Many visualization libraries offer built-in support for dynamic updates, allowing developers to update charts, graphs, and other visual elements in real-time as new data becomes available. By customizing these visualizations, developers can create dynamic and interactive user interfaces that respond to changes in the underlying data.

One popular choice for customizing data visualization in dynamic scenarios is D3.js (Data-Driven Documents), a powerful JavaScript library for creating interactive and dynamic visualizations in web applications. With D3.js, developers have full control over every aspect of the visualization, including data binding, element creation, styling, and animation. By leveraging the flexibility of D3.js, developers can create custom visualizations that update dynamically based on incoming data streams.

Another approach to customizing data visualization for dynamic updates is to use charting libraries or frameworks that offer built-in support for real-time data streams. Libraries like Chart.js, Highcharts, and Plotly provide APIs for updating charts in real-time, making it easier for developers to create dynamic visualizations without extensive customizations. These libraries often support various chart types, including line charts, bar charts, pie charts, and scatter plots, allowing developers to choose the most suitable visualization for their data.

When customizing data visualization for dynamic updates, developers may need to consider performance optimizations to ensure smooth and responsive user experiences, especially when dealing with large datasets or high-frequency updates. Techniques such as data aggregation, throttling, and debouncing can help reduce the computational overhead and improve the performance of dynamic visualizations.

In addition to updating the visual representation of data, developers may also need to implement features such as tooltips, labels, and annotations to provide context and enhance the interpretability of the visualizations. These interactive elements allow users to explore the data more effectively and gain deeper insights into the underlying trends and patterns.

One important consideration when customizing data visualization for dynamic updates is accessibility. Developers should ensure that dynamic visualizations are accessible to users with disabilities by providing alternative text descriptions, keyboard navigation support, and other accessibility features. This ensures that all users, regardless of their abilities, can access and interact with the visualizations effectively.

Deploying dynamic data visualizations in web applications typically involves serving the visualization code and data from a web server and rendering the visualizations in the client's web browser. This can be achieved using technologies like HTML, CSS, and JavaScript, along with server-side frameworks and APIs for fetching and processing data.

Overall, customizing data visualization for dynamic updates is essential for creating engaging and interactive user experiences in modern applications. By leveraging the capabilities of visualization libraries and frameworks, developers can create dynamic visualizations that adapt to changes in the underlying data and empower users to explore and analyze data in real-time. With careful consideration of performance, accessibility, and user experience, developers can build compelling data visualizations that drive insights and facilitate decision-making.

## Chapter 8: Integrating 3D Graphics with Java 3D

Java 3D graphics rendering is a powerful technology that allows developers to create immersive and interactive three-dimensional (3D) graphics and visualizations in Java applications. Java 3D provides a high-level API for rendering 3D scenes, enabling developers to manipulate and display complex 3D geometry, textures, lighting, and animations. By leveraging Java 3D, developers can build compelling applications ranging from interactive games and simulations to scientific visualizations and architectural walkthroughs.

At the core of Java 3D is the concept of a scene graph, which represents the hierarchical structure of the 3D scene. The scene graph consists of nodes that define various elements of the scene, such as geometry, transformations, lights, cameras, and behaviors. By organizing the scene as a graph of interconnected nodes, developers can easily manipulate and animate different parts of the scene while maintaining a coherent spatial relationship between objects.

To get started with Java 3D graphics rendering, developers typically create a canvas or a panel to serve as the rendering surface for the 3D scene. This can be achieved using Swing or JavaFX components, depending on the requirements of the application. Once the rendering surface is set up, developers can initialize the

Java 3D rendering pipeline and begin constructing the 3D scene.

One of the key features of Java 3D is its support for geometric primitives, such as points, lines, triangles, and polygons, which serve as the building blocks for creating 3D shapes and models. Developers can define geometric primitives directly or import 3D models from external file formats, such as OBJ, STL, or COLLADA, using libraries like Java 3D Utils or third-party loaders.

In addition to geometric primitives, Java 3D supports textures, materials, and shaders for adding visual realism to 3D objects. Textures can be applied to surfaces to simulate different materials, such as wood, metal, or fabric, while materials define properties such as color, reflectivity, and shininess. Shaders allow developers to create custom rendering effects, such as reflections, refractions, and specular highlights, by writing custom shader programs in languages like GLSL (OpenGL Shading Language).

Another important aspect of Java 3D graphics rendering is lighting, which plays a crucial role in determining the appearance of 3D scenes. Java 3D supports various types of lights, including directional lights, point lights, spotlights, and ambient lights, which can be positioned and oriented within the scene to achieve different lighting effects. By adjusting parameters such as intensity, color, and attenuation, developers can create realistic lighting environments that enhance the visual quality of the 3D scene.

To animate objects in Java 3D, developers can use transformations and behaviors to change the position, orientation, and scale of objects over time. Transformations allow developers to apply translations, rotations, and scaling operations to nodes in the scene graph, while behaviors enable dynamic interactions, such as user-controlled movement, collision detection, and procedural animations.

Java 3D also provides support for advanced rendering techniques, such as fog, depth of field, and shadow mapping, which further enhance the realism and immersion of 3D scenes. These techniques can be used to simulate atmospheric effects, simulate the focus of a camera lens, and create realistic shadows cast by objects in the scene.

Deploying Java 3D applications typically involves packaging the application code and resources into executable JAR files or Java Web Start applications, which can be distributed and run on any platform that supports Java. Developers can use build tools like Apache Maven or Gradle to automate the build process and manage dependencies, ensuring that the application is easy to deploy and maintain.

Overall, Java 3D graphics rendering provides a powerful platform for creating immersive and interactive 3D applications in Java. By leveraging its high-level API and advanced rendering capabilities, developers can build visually stunning applications that engage users and deliver compelling experiences across a wide range of domains and industries. Whether it's building games, simulations, or scientific visualizations, Java 3D offers the tools and flexibility needed to bring 3D ideas to life.

Creating interactive 3D scenes with Java 3D opens up a world of possibilities for developers looking to build engaging and immersive applications. Java 3D provides a robust framework for constructing dynamic and interactive 3D environments, allowing developers to create everything from simple games and simulations to complex scientific visualizations and architectural walkthroughs.

At the heart of Java 3D is the concept of a scene graph, which represents the hierarchical structure of the 3D scene. The scene graph consists of nodes that define various elements of the scene, such as geometry, transformations, lights, cameras, and behaviors. By organizing the scene as a graph of interconnected nodes, developers can easily manipulate and animate different parts of the scene while maintaining a coherent spatial relationship between objects.

To begin creating interactive 3D scenes with Java 3D, developers typically start by setting up the rendering environment and defining the basic components of the scene. This involves creating a canvas or panel to serve as the rendering surface for the 3D scene and initializing the Java 3D rendering pipeline. Once the rendering surface is set up, developers can begin constructing the scene by adding nodes to the scene graph.

One of the first steps in creating an interactive 3D scene is defining the geometry of the objects in the scene. Java 3D provides support for geometric primitives such as points, lines, triangles, and polygons, which serve as the building blocks for creating 3D shapes and models.

Developers can define geometric primitives directly or import 3D models from external file formats using libraries like Java 3D Utils or third-party loaders.

In addition to defining geometry, developers can add textures, materials, and shaders to objects in the scene to enhance their visual appearance. Textures can be applied to surfaces to simulate different materials, while materials define properties such as color, reflectivity, and shininess. Shaders allow developers to create custom rendering effects by writing custom shader programs in languages like GLSL.

Once the basic components of the scene are defined, developers can add lights and cameras to the scene to control the lighting and viewpoint. Java 3D supports various types of lights, including directional lights, point lights, spotlights, and ambient lights, which can be positioned and oriented within the scene to achieve different lighting effects. Cameras define the viewpoint from which the scene is rendered and can be used to control the perspective and field of view of the rendered image.

To make the scene interactive, developers can add behaviors to objects in the scene to enable dynamic interactions such as user-controlled movement, collision detection, and procedural animations. Behaviors are special types of nodes in the scene graph that respond to events and update the state of the scene accordingly. For example, a behavior might respond to keyboard or mouse input to move a character or object within the scene.

Java 3D also provides support for advanced rendering techniques such as fog, depth of field, and shadow mapping, which can be used to enhance the realism and immersion of 3D scenes. These techniques can be used to simulate atmospheric effects, simulate the focus of a camera lens, and create realistic shadows cast by objects in the scene.

Deploying interactive 3D scenes created with Java 3D typically involves packaging the application code and resources into executable JAR files or Java Web Start applications, which can be distributed and run on any platform that supports Java. Developers can use build tools like Apache Maven or Gradle to automate the build process and manage dependencies, ensuring that the application is easy to deploy and maintain.

In summary, Java 3D provides a powerful platform for creating interactive 3D scenes in Java. By leveraging its high-level API and advanced rendering capabilities, developers can build visually stunning applications that engage users and deliver compelling experiences across a wide range of domains and industries. Whether it's building games, simulations, or scientific visualizations, Java 3D offers the tools and flexibility needed to bring interactive 3D scenes to life.

## Chapter 9: Secure GUI Applications with Java Security Features

Implementing code signing and security policies is essential for ensuring the integrity and safety of software applications in today's digital landscape. Code signing involves digitally signing executable files and scripts to verify their authenticity and integrity, while security policies define rules and restrictions to protect against unauthorized access and malicious activities. By combining these techniques, developers can establish a robust security framework to safeguard their software and protect users from potential threats.

To implement code signing, developers typically use cryptographic algorithms to generate digital signatures for their code. This process involves using a private key to sign the code and a corresponding public key to verify the signature. The most common algorithm used for code signing is RSA (Rivest-Shamir-Adleman), which provides strong security guarantees against tampering and forgery.

In Java, code signing is often performed using the jarsigner tool, which is included with the Java Development Kit (JDK). To sign a Java Archive (JAR) file, developers can use the following command:

bashCopy code

```
jarsigner -keystore keystore_file jar_file alias
```

This command prompts the user to enter the password for the keystore file and then signs the JAR file with the specified alias. The keystore file contains the developer's private key and certificates, which are used to generate the digital signature.

In addition to code signing, developers can also enforce security policies to control access to their applications and protect sensitive resources. Security policies define rules and permissions that specify which users or groups are allowed to perform certain actions within the application. For example, developers can restrict access to certain features or functionalities based on user roles or privileges.

In Java, security policies are typically configured using the java.policy file, which specifies the permissions granted to code running within the Java Virtual Machine (JVM). Developers can define custom security policies by editing the java.policy file directly or by using the policytool utility, which provides a graphical interface for managing security policies.

To edit the java.policy file using the policytool utility, developers can use the following command:

Copy code

```
policytool
```

This command opens the policytool GUI, where developers can add, remove, or modify security policies for different code sources and permissions. Developers can specify permissions such as file access, network access, and runtime privileges, allowing fine-grained control over the security configuration of their applications.

In addition to code signing and security policies, developers can also implement other security measures such as encryption, authentication, and access control to further enhance the security of their applications. Encryption involves encoding data using cryptographic algorithms to protect it from unauthorized access or tampering, while authentication verifies the identity of users or entities accessing the application.

Access control mechanisms such as role-based access control (RBAC) and attribute-based access control (ABAC) allow developers to define rules and policies governing access to resources based on user roles, attributes, or other contextual information. By implementing these security measures, developers can mitigate security risks and ensure the confidentiality, integrity, and availability of their software applications.

Deploying code-signed and securely configured applications involves distributing the signed executable files or scripts along with any necessary configuration files or resources. Developers should ensure that the code signing certificates and keystore files are securely stored and managed to prevent unauthorized access or misuse. Additionally, developers should regularly update and review their security policies to address emerging threats and vulnerabilities.

In summary, implementing code signing and security policies is essential for ensuring the integrity and security of software applications. By digitally signing executable files and scripts and enforcing security policies, developers can protect their applications against unauthorized access, tampering, and other malicious activities. By combining these techniques with other security measures such as encryption, authentication, and access control, developers can establish a robust security framework to safeguard their software and protect users from potential threats.

Securing user data and application resources is paramount in modern software development, especially considering the increasing frequency of cyber threats and data breaches. Developers must employ robust security measures to protect sensitive information and prevent unauthorized access to valuable resources. This entails implementing encryption, access controls, secure authentication mechanisms, and auditing capabilities to ensure the confidentiality, integrity, and availability of user data and application resources.

One of the fundamental principles of securing user data is encryption, which involves converting plaintext information into ciphertext using cryptographic algorithms. This process ensures that even if attackers gain unauthorized access to the data, they cannot decipher its contents without the appropriate decryption key. Developers can use encryption techniques such as symmetric encryption, where the same key is used for both encryption and decryption, or asymmetric encryption, where different keys are used for encryption and decryption. The openssl command-line tool is often used to perform encryption and decryption tasks. For example, to encrypt a file using symmetric encryption with AES-256:

csharpCopy code

```
openssl enc -aes-256-cbc -in input.txt -out encrypted.txt
```

To decrypt the encrypted file:

csharpCopy code

```
openssl enc -d -aes-256-cbc -in encrypted.txt -out decrypted.txt
```

Access controls are another critical aspect of securing user data and application resources. Access control mechanisms allow developers to define and enforce permissions for accessing sensitive data and functionalities based on user roles, privileges, or other attributes. Role-based access control (RBAC) and attribute-based access control (ABAC) are common access control models used to manage user access to resources. RBAC assigns roles to users and grants permissions based on those roles, while ABAC evaluates attributes and policies to determine access rights. Access controls can be implemented programmatically within the application code or through dedicated access control frameworks and libraries.

Secure authentication mechanisms are essential for verifying the identity of users and ensuring that only authorized individuals can access the application and its resources. Techniques such as username/password authentication, multi-factor authentication (MFA), and biometric authentication help authenticate users securely. Additionally, developers should employ best practices such as salting and hashing passwords to protect user credentials from being compromised in the event of a data breach.

Auditing capabilities play a crucial role in monitoring and tracking user activities within the application. Auditing allows developers to record and analyze user interactions, access attempts, and system events to detect suspicious behavior, identify security incidents, and comply with regulatory requirements. Audit logs should capture relevant information such as user actions, timestamps, IP addresses, and resource access details. Tools like the Elastic Stack (formerly known as the ELK stack), which includes Elasticsearch, Logstash, and Kibana, can be used to collect, store, and analyze audit logs effectively.

Deploying secure user data and application resource protection involves integrating these security measures seamlessly into the software development lifecycle. Developers should conduct thorough security assessments and risk analyses to identify potential vulnerabilities and threats. Security testing techniques such as penetration testing, vulnerability scanning, and code reviews help identify and remediate security flaws before deployment. Additionally, developers should stay abreast of emerging security trends, vulnerabilities, and best practices to adapt their security strategies accordingly.

Continuous monitoring and proactive threat detection are essential for maintaining the security posture of the application post-deployment. Security monitoring tools and intrusion detection systems (IDS) can help detect and respond to security incidents in real-time, minimizing the impact of potential breaches. Regular security audits and compliance assessments ensure that the application remains compliant with industry standards and regulatory requirements.

In summary, securing user data and application resources is a multifaceted process that requires a comprehensive approach encompassing encryption, access controls, secure authentication mechanisms, auditing capabilities, and continuous monitoring. By implementing these security measures effectively and integrating them into the software development lifecycle, developers can protect sensitive information, prevent unauthorized access, and mitigate the risks posed by cyber threats and data breaches.

## Chapter 10: Building Extensible and Scalable Swing Applications

Design patterns play a crucial role in software development, providing reusable solutions to common design problems and promoting maintainability, flexibility, and extensibility in applications. In the context of Swing applications, leveraging design patterns can significantly enhance the architecture and facilitate the development of modular, scalable, and extensible solutions.

One of the most widely used design patterns in Swing applications is the Model-View-Controller (MVC) pattern, which separates the application into three distinct components: the model, the view, and the controller. The model represents the application's data and business logic, the view displays the user interface elements, and the controller handles user input and updates the model accordingly. By decoupling these components, the MVC pattern enables easier maintenance, testing, and extensibility of Swing applications. Developers can use the **javax.swing** package to implement the MVC pattern effectively, with classes such as **JFrame** representing the view, custom model classes for the model, and event listeners for the controller.

Another essential design pattern for extensibility in Swing applications is the Observer pattern, which establishes a one-to-many dependency between objects, allowing multiple observers to be notified of changes to a subject's state. In Swing, the Observer pattern is commonly used to handle event-driven programming, where components such as buttons, text fields, and menus generate events that are observed and handled by listener objects. For example, the ActionListener interface in Swing serves as an observer for button click events, enabling developers to implement custom event handling logic by registering ActionListener objects with buttons using the **addActionListener()** method.

The Command pattern is another valuable design pattern for extensibility in Swing applications, encapsulating requests as objects and allowing them to be parameterized, queued, or logged for later execution. In Swing, commands can be represented as Action objects, which encapsulate user actions such as button clicks, menu selections, or keyboard shortcuts. By encapsulating actions as objects, developers can easily extend and modify the behavior of Swing components without modifying their implementation. The **javax.swing.Action** interface provides a standard way to define custom actions and bind them to Swing components using the **setAction()** method.

The Strategy pattern is also beneficial for extensibility in Swing applications, allowing developers to define a family of algorithms, encapsulate them into separate classes, and make them interchangeable at runtime. In Swing, the Strategy pattern is often used to customize the behavior of components such as layout managers, rendering strategies, and input validation mechanisms.

For example, developers can implement custom layout managers by subclassing the LayoutManager interface and overriding its methods to define the layout algorithm. Then, they can configure Swing containers to use the custom layout manager by calling the **setLayout()** method with an instance of the custom layout manager class.

The Factory Method pattern is particularly useful for extensibility in Swing applications, providing a way to encapsulate object creation logic in a separate method or class and allowing subclasses to override the creation process to produce objects of different types. In Swing, developers can use the Factory Method pattern to create instances of Swing components dynamically based on runtime conditions or configuration parameters. For example, developers can define a factory class that encapsulates the creation logic for different types of buttons and use it to create instances of specific button subclasses such as JButton, JToggleButton, or JCheckBox.

Additionally, the Decorator pattern can enhance extensibility in Swing applications by dynamically adding or modifying behavior of Swing components at runtime without altering their underlying implementation. Decorator classes wrap existing Swing components and provide additional functionality by intercepting method calls, executing custom logic, and delegating to the wrapped component. For example, developers can create custom decorators to add features such as tooltip support, custom painting, or event handling to

Swing components without subclassing or modifying the original components.

In summary, leveraging design patterns such as MVC, Observer, Command, Strategy, Factory Method, and Decorator can significantly enhance the extensibility of Swing applications, enabling developers to build modular, maintainable, and flexible solutions that can adapt to changing requirements and accommodate future enhancements. By understanding and applying these design patterns effectively, developers can create robust and scalable Swing applications that meet the needs of users and stakeholders alike. Scaling Swing applications to handle large datasets and user bases is a critical aspect of software development, especially in scenarios where the application needs to accommodate a growing number of users or process large volumes of data efficiently. This topic delves into various techniques and best practices for optimizing Swing applications to ensure optimal performance and responsiveness even when dealing with extensive datasets and user loads.

One fundamental aspect of scaling Swing applications is optimizing the handling of large datasets. When dealing with a significant amount of data, efficient data retrieval, storage, and processing are crucial for maintaining application responsiveness. One approach is to leverage pagination and lazy loading techniques to fetch data in smaller chunks rather than loading the entire dataset at once. By fetching data incrementally,

developers can reduce memory usage and improve application responsiveness, especially in scenarios where users interact with a subset of the data at a time. To implement pagination and lazy loading in a Swing application, developers can use libraries such as Hibernate for database access or implement custom data retrieval logic. For example, when displaying large datasets in tables or lists, developers can fetch a limited number of records initially and load additional records as the user scrolls or navigates through the dataset. This approach ensures that only the data required for immediate display is loaded into memory, minimizing memory usage and improving application performance.
Another technique for scaling Swing applications is optimizing the rendering and processing of user interface components. When dealing with large datasets, rendering complex user interface components such as tables, trees, or charts can impact application performance, especially on older hardware or devices with limited resources. To mitigate this, developers can implement virtual rendering techniques to render only the visible portion of large components, reducing rendering overhead and improving overall application performance.

Virtual rendering techniques involve dynamically rendering only the visible portion of a user interface component while maintaining the appearance of a complete dataset. For example, when displaying a large table with thousands of rows, developers can implement virtual scrolling to render only the rows

visible within the viewport and dynamically load additional rows as the user scrolls. This approach minimizes memory usage and rendering overhead, resulting in a smoother user experience, even when dealing with extensive datasets.
Furthermore, optimizing data processing and computation is essential for scaling Swing applications. When performing complex calculations or data manipulation operations on large datasets, developers should strive to minimize processing time and resource usage to ensure optimal application performance. One approach is to leverage multithreading and parallel processing techniques to distribute computation across multiple threads or processor cores, enabling concurrent execution of tasks and maximizing hardware utilization.

To implement multithreading and parallel processing in Swing applications, developers can use Java's built-in concurrency utilities such as the Executor framework or Java's Fork/Join framework. By offloading time-consuming tasks such as data processing, computation, or I/O operations to background threads, developers can prevent blocking the event dispatch thread (EDT) and ensure that the user interface remains responsive and fluid, even when performing resource-intensive operations.

Additionally, optimizing memory usage and resource management is crucial for scaling Swing applications. When dealing with large datasets, inefficient memory management practices such as excessive object creation, memory leaks, or unnecessary resource retention can lead to memory exhaustion and degraded application performance. To mitigate this, developers should employ techniques such as object pooling, resource caching, and memory profiling to identify and address memory bottlenecks and resource inefficiencies.

Object pooling involves reusing objects instead of creating new ones, reducing memory allocation overhead and garbage collection pressure. By pooling frequently used objects such as database connections, thread pools, or data structures, developers can minimize memory churn and improve application performance. Similarly, caching frequently accessed resources such as database queries, computed results, or frequently used images can reduce redundant computation and improve application responsiveness.

Memory profiling tools such as Java's VisualVM or third-party profilers can help developers identify memory leaks, excessive object creation, and other memory-related issues in Swing applications. By analyzing memory usage patterns, object lifecycles, and memory allocation traces, developers can pinpoint memory bottlenecks and optimize memory usage to ensure efficient resource utilization and optimal application performance.

In summary, scaling Swing applications for large datasets and user bases requires careful optimization of data retrieval, rendering, processing, memory usage, and resource management. By implementing techniques such as pagination, lazy loading, virtual rendering, multithreading, parallel processing, object pooling, resource caching, and memory profiling, developers can optimize Swing applications to handle extensive datasets and user loads efficiently while maintaining optimal performance and responsiveness.

## Conclusion

In summary, the Java Swing Programming bundle offers a comprehensive journey from novice to expert in graphical user interface (GUI) programming using Java Swing. Beginning with "Java Swing Essentials," readers are introduced to the fundamental concepts and components of Swing, laying a strong foundation for GUI development. "Mastering Java Swing" takes intermediate users to the next level with advanced techniques and elegant interface design principles, enhancing their skills in creating polished and user-friendly applications.

Moving forward, "Advanced Java Swing Development" delves into building dynamic and responsive GUIs, exploring topics such as data visualization, event handling, and customization for complex applications. Finally, "Expert-level Java Swing Mastery" provides in-depth insights and advanced strategies for harnessing the full power of GUI programming, empowering developers to create sophisticated and professional-grade applications.

Through these four books, readers embark on a progressive learning journey, gradually advancing from beginner to expert level in Java Swing programming. Whether you are a novice looking to enter the world of GUI development or an experienced developer seeking to refine your skills, this bundle equips you with the knowledge and techniques needed to excel in Java Swing programming and create stunning, feature-rich applications with confidence.

www.ingramcontent.com/pod-product-compliance
Lightning Source LLC
Chambersburg PA
CBHW070936050326
40689CB00014B/3226

* 9 7 8 1 8 3 9 3 8 7 3 4 0 *